Vegan College Cookbook

Vegan College Cookbook

Easy, Healthy, and Delicious Vegan Recipes for Students and More

Amanda Baines

DYLANNAPRESS

First edition: 2017

Disclaimer/Limit of Liability
This book is for informational purposes only. The views expressed are those of the author alone,
and should not be taken as expert, legal, or medical advice. The reader is responsible for his or her own actions.
Every attempt has been made to verify the accuracy of the information in this publication. However, neither the author nor the
publisher assumes any responsibility for errors, omissions, or contrary interpretation of the material contained herein.
This book is not intended to provide medical advice. Please see your health care professional before embarking on any new
diet or exercise program. The reader should regularly consult a physician in matters relating to his/her health and particularly
with respect to any symptoms that may require diagnosis or medical attention.
This book is not endorsed by or affiliated with the NuWave Oven corporation.
All trademarks are property of their respective owners.

Photo credits: Shutterstock

CONTENTS

Smoothies   45

Salads   57

Sweets 161

INTRODUCTION

The *College Vegan Cookbook* was designed specifically for busy college students like you who want to eat a healthy vegan diet without spending a fortune or countless hours in the kitchen. It is full of delicious and inexpensive meals you can whip up in no time whether you are a novice in the kitchen or an experienced cook.

We know that it can be hard to eat healthy in college, especially vegan, given time, budget, and kitchen constraints and this cookbook was designed to show you that preparing fresh, homemade, vegan meals does not have to be hard or expensive. You can make a surprising amount of delicious meals even on a tight budget or in a limited space. So what are you waiting for? Let's get cooking!

STOCKING YOUR KITCHEN

WHETHER big or small, having a few basics on hand in your kitchen will make it a lot easier to whip together healthy snacks and meals when you're hungry.

Basic Tools and Equipment

You don't need a lot of expensive appliances or fancy ingredients to make great-tasting vegan dishes, but it helps to have a few basic kitchen supplies and pantry essentials on hand.

- **Knives** – a few good knives will make your time in the kitchen much easier
  - Chef's knife
  - Paring knife
  - Serrated knife
- **Cutting boards**
- **Can opener**
- **Colander**
- **Liquid measuring cup**
- **Measuring spoons**
- **Tongs**
- **Garlic press** (not essential but very handy)
- **Vegetable peeler**

- **Spoons**
  - Wooden spoon
  - Large slotted spoon
- **Spatula**
- **Ladle**
- **Large pot** (for cooking pasta, soups)
- **Saucepan**, 3-quart
- **Skillets** – A 12-inch and an 8-inch, nonstick
- **Mixing bowls**

Depending on your space and budget, a few other nice-to-have kitchen items include:

- **Toaster oven**
- **Coffee maker**
- **Slow cooker**
- **Mini food processor**
- **Blender**
- **Microwave**
- **Grater**
- **Immersion blender**

When stocking your kitchen don't forget the clean-up and storage supplies:

- **Dish soap**
- **Sponges**
- **Paper towels**
- **Dish towels**

- **Plastic wrap**
- **Resealable bags**
- **Aluminum foil**
- **Storage containers for leftovers**

Ingredients to Have on Hand

A well-stocked pantry, refrigerator, and freezer makes preparing a meal much easier. Keep these basics on hand and you'll always be able cook up a quick healthy meal or snack.

Pantry Items

- **Nut butters** – Almond, cashew, peanut butter

- **Canned beans, dried beans** – Black beans, kidney beans, chickpeas, pinto beans, lentils, cannellini

- **Pasta** – It's nice to have a variety of dried pasta on hand including elbows, spaghetti, rigatoni, shells. Some vegan pasta brands include Barilla, Bertolli, De Cecco, Kroger, Ronzoni, Safeway, and Trader Joe's.

- **Rice** – White and brown

- **Ramen noodles** – Ramen noodles themselves are vegan; it's the seasoning packs you need to watch out for. One exception we've found, Top Ramen Oriental Flavor contains no animal ingredients. Otherwise, throw out the seasoning packet and add your own spices.

- **Oatmeal** – Instant, quick cooking, steel cut

- **Tortillas** – Corn, flour

- **Canned tomatoes** – Diced, whole, crushed, and paste

- **Spaghetti sauce** – Check the ingredients to make sure its vegan. Some to try include Classico marinara, spicy red pepper, tomato & basil; Prego garlic and basil; Newman's Own cabernet marinara

- **Oils** – Olive, coconut, canola, peanut, sesame seed

- **Vinegar** – Apple cider, balsamic, red wine

- **Black pepper** – Get one with a built-in grinder

- **Salt** – Sea salt, kosher salt, Himalayan salt

- **Flour** – All purpose, whole-wheat

- **Sugar** – White, brown

- **Maple syrup**

- **Nutritional yeast** – Adds a cheesy flavor to dishes

- **Herbs and spices** – Basil, bay leaf, black pepper, cayenne pepper, cinnamon, cumin, curry, coriander, garlic powder/salt, ginger, oregano, rosemary, thyme,

- **Salad dressing** – Check the ingredients to make sure it's vegan.

- **Condiments** – Vegan mayo, Dijon mustard

- **Soy sauce**

Refrigerator and Freezer Items

- **Coconut and/or almond milk**

- **Vegan butter**

- **Fruits** – Apples, oranges, bananas, berries, lemons, limes

- **Salad greens**

- **Carrots**

- **Celery**

- **Onions**

- **Garlic**

- **Potatoes**

- **Juice**

- **Hummus**

- **Bread**

- **Frozen vegetables**

- **Yogurt** – Soy or coconut milk

Now that your kitchen is stocked it's time to get cooking!

BREAKFAST

Breakfast is said to be the most important meal of the day and not to be missed. Whether you need to eat it on the go on the way to class, can enjoy a long leisurely Sunday meal, or something in between, this chapter provides lots of nutritious and delicious options for your morning meal.

Overnight Cinnamon Apple Oatmeal

Super easy out-the-door breakfast.

Servings: 1

¾ cup of oats

¾ cup of almond milk (or any other vegan milk of your choice!)

1 tablespoon chia seeds

½ tablespoon maple syrup

½ teaspoon ground cinnamon

¼ teaspoon vanilla extract

¼ cup of water

½ apple

1. In a mason jar or other large glass container add oats, almond milk, chia seeds, maple syrup, cinnamon, vanilla extract, and water.

2. Stir thoroughly and place in refrigerator overnight.

3. The next morning, chop up apple, toss into oatmeal, and enjoy!

Breakfast Cookie in a Mug

Quick and creative 5-minute breakfast!

Servings: 1

½ **of a large banana**

1 ½ **tablespoons almond or peanut butter**

½ **tablespoon maple syrup or agave**

1 **tablespoon almond milk**

4 **tablespoon oats**

1 **tablespoon of dried cranberries or raisins**

1. In a large microwave-safe mug, mash your banana with a fork.

2. Add almond/peanut butter, almond milk, and maple syrup/agave. Stir.

3. Add oats and cranberries or raisins.

4. Stir until all ingredients are combined.

5. Microwave for 45 seconds (or until it is firm to the touch).

6. Enjoy!

Banana Bread Mug Cake

Filling and tasty breakfast treat.

Servings: 1

½ banana

1 tablespoon sugar

2 tablespoons flour

1/8 teaspoon baking powder

1/8 teaspoon cinnamon

½ teaspoon coconut oil

¼ teaspoon vanilla extract

1 teaspoon dairy-free chocolate chips (optional)

1 teaspoon walnuts, chopped (optional)

1. Mash banana in a microwave-safe bowl. Add all other ingredients besides chocolate chips and walnuts, and mix until smooth.

2. Stir in half of the walnuts and chocolate chips. Sprinkle remaining on top.

3. Put mug in microwave for 90 seconds. Enjoy!

Tofu Scramble in a Mug

Easy tofu scramble you can make in the microwave!

Servings: 1

½ block crumbled tofu

½ cup nutritional yeast

1 tablespoon soy sauce

½ tablespoon lemon juice

½ cup spinach

¼ cup mushrooms

Seasonings (optional)

1. Add all ingredients into a microwave safe bowl and microwave for 60 seconds. Stir and enjoy.

Overnight Blueberry Maple Oatmeal

Wake up to a delicious breakfast

Servings: 1

¼ cup oats

1/3 cup almond milk

¼ cup vegan yogurt

1 ½ tablespoons of chia seeds

2 teaspoons maple syrup

¼ cup blueberries

1. In a mason jar add oats, almond milk, yogurt, chia seeds, and maple syrup.

2. Secure jar and shake until all is combined.

3. Add blueberries and mix.

4. Put in refrigerator overnight and serve the next morning.

Healthy Low-Fat Granola

Making your own granola is very easy and economical.

Servings: 4

2 cups old fashioned oats

1/8 cup flax seed

1/8 cup wheat germ

1/8 cup coconut flakes

1/8 cup sunflower seeds

¼ cup sliced almonds

1/6 cup maple syrup

1/8 cup apple juice

½ teaspoon cinnamon

½ teaspoon vanilla

1/8 teaspoon salt

1. In a large bowl, combine all ingredients. Stir well to thoroughly coat all ingredients.

2. Line rimmed cookie sheet with parchment paper. Spread mixture evenly on cookie sheet.

3. Place pan in oven, cook at 350 degrees F for 10 minutes.

4. Take out pan, stir, and cook for an additional 10-15 minutes, until lightly brown.

5. Allow to cool, and store in airtight container.

Vegan Breakfast Sandwich

Very filling, healthy, and affordable breakfast for on the go!

1 English muffin

1 tablespoon hummus

¼ cup of scrambled tofu

1 strip of vegan bacon, cooked

Sprinkle of vegan cheese alternative

1 slice of tomato

1 slice of avocado

1. Toast your English muffin.

2. Spread each side with hummus or guacamole.

3. Layer scrambled tofu, vegan bacon, vegan cheese, tomato, and avocado on one side of the English muffin.

4. Top with other half of English muffin and put it in the microwave for 30 seconds.

5. Enjoy!

Peanut Butter and Banana Oatmeal

This will keep you fueled all morning.

Servings: 1

1 mashed banana

2 tablespoons of peanut butter

½ cup of instant oatmeal

Splash of almond milk

Salt to taste

Cinnamon as garnish

Berries of your choice

1. In a mug, mash a banana. Add in peanut butter and stir in oatmeal.

2. Add a splash of almond milk and mix. Press down mixture until flat

3. Microwave for 2 minutes

4. Garnish with cinnamon and berries of your choice.

Microwave Peanut Butter Pancakes

Unique and interesting meal that can be used as a breakfast, snack, or lunch!

Servings: 2

½ cup peanut flour

½ tablespoon stevia (Truvia)

1 tablespoon vanilla protein powder

¼ teaspoon baking powder

1/8 teaspoon cinnamon

Dash of salt

½ cup applesauce

1 tablespoon Silk yogurt

1/8 teaspoon vanilla extract

¼ teaspoon apple cider vinegar

1. In a bowl, mix together all dry ingredients.

2. In a separate bowl, whisk all wet ingredients together.

3. Pour wet ingredient mixture over the dry mixture, stir until combined, and let it stand for 5 minutes.

4. Spray a microwaveable plate with cooking spray and spread ½ of the batter on the plate so that it is 1 inch thick

5. Microwave it for 40 seconds and then repeat with the rest of the batter.

6. Serve topped with maple syrup and berries.

Breakfast Pizza

Pizza for breakfast? You bet!

Servings: 3-4

12-inch pizza crust of your choice

8 pieces of tempeh bacon

2/3 cup of pizza sauce

2/3 cup of vegan mozzarella (Daiya or similar)

1 cup tofu scramble (page 23)

1 sliced tomato

Oregano, crushed red pepper flakes, and salt to taste

1. Cook bacon according to instructions, remove from pan, and cut into pieces.

2. Spread pizza sauce over crust and sprinkle with cheese. Top with tofu scramble, bacon, and tomato slices.

3. Add remaining cheese, then sprinkle with oregano, red pepper flakes, and salt and pepper.

4. Bake for 14-16 minutes at 425 degrees or until cheese has melted.

5. Cut and serve!

Coconut, Fruit, and Nut Granola

Healthy and crunchy snack or breakfast!

Servings: 4

¼ cup melted coconut oil

¼ cup maple syrup

1 ½ cups unsweetened coconut flakes

1 cup almonds, roughly chopped

½ cup sunflower seeds, raw

2 tablespoons chia seeds

¼ cup almond meal

¼ cup dried fruit (Ex: raisins, dried plums, cranberries, banana chips, mango)

1. Line a cookie sheet with parchment paper.

2. In a large mixing bowl, combine the melted coconut oil and honey or maple syrup. Add all other ingredients in except for dried fruit. Mix well to combine and thoroughly coat all ingredients.

3. Spread mixture onto a cookie sheet into a thin layer. Bake in preheated 325 F-degree oven for 20 minutes, remove tray from oven and flip mixture over with spatula. Return to oven and cook for another 20 minutes or until it is golden brown.

4. Remove from oven and sprinkle with dried fruit. Allow to cool. Can be stored in an airtight container for up to a week.

Coconut-Banana "Oatmeal"

Yummy and interesting breakfast you can make in the microwave!

Servings: 1

1 banana

2 tablespoons coconut butter

½ teaspoon cinnamon

Sea salt to taste

Blueberries as topping

1. In a small bowl, mash banana. Add salt and cinnamon.

2. In a microwave safe bowl, heat coconut oil for 30 seconds.

3. Add coconut butter to banana mixture and stir.

4. Top with blueberries or other fruit.

Breakfast Burrito

Satisfying and healthy breakfast

Servings: 2

1 tablespoon olive oil

2 white mushrooms, sliced

1 clove garlic, minced

1/8 cup red onion, diced

¼ red pepper, diced

½ package pressed tofu, crumbled

½ teaspoon each: cumin, chili powder, salt, pepper, garlic powder, and turmeric mixed with 2 teaspoons of water

2 flour tortilla wraps

Additional toppings: Lime juice, lettuce, salsa, refried beans (heated), avocado, fresh cilantro

1. Heat oil in skillet over medium heat.

2. Add in garlic, red onion, mushrooms, and red pepper. Cook until the onions and mushrooms start to soften, 4-5 minutes.

3. Add in crumbled tofu and spice mixture. Stir well and mix until all tofu is heated through, 2-3 minutes.

4. Divide mixture evenly between the two wraps. Top with additional toppings of your choice.

Breakfast Quinoa

Hearty and healthy breakfast!

Servings: 1

1/8 cup raw almonds, chopped

½ cup quinoa

½ teaspoon. ground cinnamon

1 cup of almond milk

½ teaspoon salt

1 dried pitted date, finely chopped

2 dried apricots, finely chopped

½ teaspoon. vanilla extract

1 tablespoon maple syrup

1. In skillet, toast almonds for about 4 minutes or until golden brown. Set aside.

2. In the same pan, combine quinoa and cinnamon, and heat over medium flame for several seconds until heated through. Mix in almond milk and salt; bring to a boil, reduce heat to low and simmer about 15 minutes. Stir in remaining ingredients.

3. Serve with some additional almonds on top, if desired.

Tomato and Basil Avocado Toast

Simple breakfast full of healthy fats.

Servings: 1

1 slice of whole grain toast

½ of an avocado, mashed

2-3 leaves fresh basil, chopped

5 cherry tomatoes, halved

Salt and freshly ground black pepper, to taste

Balsamic vinegar

1. Spread mashed avocado on top of your toast.

2. Top with fresh chopped basil, and cherry tomatoes. Season with salt, pepper, and drizzle of balsamic vinegar.

Cherry Quinoa Porridge

A porridge rich in dried cherries and quinoa.

Servings: 1

¼ cup dry quinoa

¼ cup dried cherries, unsweetened

½ cup water

1/8 teaspoon ground cinnamon

¼ teaspoon vanilla extract

½ tablespoon maple syrup

1. In saucepan, combine all ingredients and cook over medium heat until boiling. Lower heat, cover, and simmer for about 15 minutes or until quinoa has softened and most of the liquid is absorbed.

2. Place in serving bowl and drizzle with extra maple syrup, if desired. Enjoy!

Banana-Pear Breakfast Medley

½ large banana

½ large ripe pear

¼ teaspoon cinnamon

Juice from 1 lime wedge

1. Peel banana and slice into round pieces, place in a bowl.

2. Peel pear and cut into small chunks, place in a bowl with banana. Sprinkle with cinnamon and mix to coat.

3. Add lime juice and mix again. Let marinate for 10 minutes before serving.

Easy Vegan French Toast

For a special treat try this quick and easy breakfast.

Servings: 2

2 tablespoons almond flour

1 teaspoon cinnamon

½ cup coconut milk (or almond milk)

2 tablespoons orange juice

1 teaspoon vanilla extract

¼ teaspoon salt

1 tablespoon vegetable oil or vegan butter

4 slices thick-cut bread

Toppings of choice: Berries, banana slices, maple syrup, cinnamon-sugar

1. In a shallow bowl, whisk together almond flour, cinnamon, coconut milk, orange, vanilla extract, and salt.

2. Heat oil or butter in skillet over medium-high heat.

3. Dip each slice of bread in mixture, turning to coat both sides. Place in skillet and cook until golden brown, 2-3 minutes. Turn over and cook until golden brown on other side. This may need to be done in batches, depending on size of pan.

4. Serve warm with topping of your choice.

Apple-Cinnamon Muffins

These muffins can be made ahead for a quick grab-and-go breakfast.

Servings: 12 muffins

1 ½ cups all-purpose flour

½ cup whole wheat flour

1 ½ teaspoon baking powder

½ teaspoon baking soda

2 teaspoons cinnamon

½ teaspoon salt

½ cup vegan butter

½ cup brown sugar

½ cup white sugar

1 ¼ cup applesauce

1 ½ teaspoon vanilla extract

1 small apple, chopped into small pieces

Sugar for sprinkling on top, if desired

1. Preheat oven to 400 degrees F. Line muffin tins with paper liners or spray with nonstick cooking spray.

2. In large mixing bowl, mix together flours, baking powder, baking soda, cinnamon, and salt.

3. In separate bowl, beat together butter, sugars, applesauce, and vanilla extract. Fold in apple pieces. Add this mixture to flour. Mix until just combined.

4. Spoon batter evenly into muffin tins. Sprinkle with sugar if using.

5. Bake for 20 minutes or until toothpick inserted in center comes out clean and tops are golden brown.

6. Serve and enjoy!

Banana-Walnut Muffins

So yummy and moist, these muffins are sure to disappear fast.

Servings: 12 muffins

2 ½ cups all-purpose flour

½ cup white sugar

½ cup brown sugar, lightly packed

1 teaspoon salt

2 teaspoons cinnamon

1 teaspoon nutmeg

1 teaspoons baking powder

1 teaspoon baking soda

1 ½ cups mashed bananas (4-5 bananas)

1 cup coconut milk

¾ cup canola oil

1. Preheat oven to 350 degrees F. Line muffins tins with paper muffin liners or spray with nonstick cooking spray.

2. In large mixing bowl, mix together flour, sugars, salt, cinnamon, nutmeg, baking powder, and baking soda.

3. In separate bowl, mix together bananas, coconut milk, and oil. Add banana mixture to flour mixture and stir until just combined. Do not over stir.

4. Scoop batter into muffin tins.

5. Bake in oven for 30 to 35 minutes or until toothpick inserted in center comes out clean.

No-Bake Granola Bars

Quick and easy, these make a great breakfast on the go or throw one in your backpack for a mid-morning or afternoon snack.

Servings: 12 bars

2 cups rolled oats

1 ½ cups natural crunchy peanut butter

1 cup ground flaxseed

¾ cup maple syrup

½ cup vegan chocolate chips

¾ cup dried cranberries

½ cup shredded coconut

¼ cup sliced almonds

1. Line a 9 x 11-inch baking sheet with wax paper.

2. In large mixing bowl, stir together oats, peanut butter, flaxseed, maple syrup, chocolate chips, coconut, and almonds.

3. Press mixture into baking sheet using back of spatula to flatten.

4. Place in refrigerator and chill for at least an hour.

5. Cut into 12 bars. Store in refrigerator until ready to eat.

Easy Vegan Pancakes

Light, fluffy, and delicious, everyone will want one!

Servings: 3

1 ½ cup all-purpose flour

2 tablespoons white sugar

½ teaspoon salt

2 teaspoons baking powder

¾ cup almond milk

½ cup water

1 tablespoon oil

Nonstick cooking spray

1. Mix together the flour, sugar, salt, and baking powder in large mixing bowl.

2. In small bowl, whisk together almond milk, water, and oil.

3. Make well in center of flour mixture and pour in wet ingredients. Stir until just blended. Batter will still be lumpy.

4. Spray large skillet with cooking spray and heat over medium-high heat. When hot, add batter in ¼ cup increments to skillet. Cook until bubbles form and edges start to dry. Flip over and cook until golden brown. Remove from skillet and continue cooking remaining batter in batches.

5. Serve topped with fresh fruit and maple syrup.

Broiled Grapefruit

Sweet and sour combine nicely in this breakfast treat.

Servings: 2

1 grapefruit, halved

¼ cup brown sugar

½ teaspoon cinnamon

1. Preheat broiler.

2. Using a sharp knife, cut around and between grapefruit segments to loosen them.

3. Combine brown sugar and cinnamon in small bowl. Sprinkle mixture over each grapefruit half.

4. Place grapefruit in baking dish and put under broiler for 2-3 minutes, until bubbling.

5. Serve at once.

SMOOTHIES

Refreshing and nutritious, a smoothie is the perfect breakfast, lunch, or snack.

Making your own is simple and economical.

Strawberry Oatmeal Smoothie

Great, easy breakfast or snack!

Servings: 1

½ cup almonds

¼ cup rolled oats

7 frozen strawberries

½ banana

¼ teaspoon vanilla extract (optional)

½ cup almond milk or water

1. Place all ingredients in a blender and blend until smooth.

2. Serve and enjoy!

Almond Butter, Coconut, and Vanilla Smoothie

Yummy and quick protein-filled breakfast or snack.

Servings: 1

½ cup coconut milk

1 tablespoon almond butter

5 small dates

½ teaspoon vanilla extract

1 cup of ice, crushed

Stevia, to taste

1. Add all ingredients to blender with ice on top and blend until smooth.

2. Serve and enjoy!

Banana Bread Smoothie

Filling and quick smoothie that can be eaten as a snack or breakfast!

Servings: 1

1 cup water

1 frozen banana

⅓ cup cooked quinoa

1 tablespoon raw walnuts

2 teaspoon flax oil

1 medjool date, pitted

½ teaspoon pure vanilla extract

¾ teaspoon cinnamon

1. Place all ingredients in blender and blend until smooth.

2. Serve and enjoy!

Energy-Packed Green Smoothie

Green tea and spinach will give you an energy boost.

Servings: 1

1 cucumber, peeled and sliced

3 cups baby spinach

½ honeydew melon, cubed

1 cup of green tea

1 teaspoon of lemon juice

½ inch of ginger root, grated

1. Add all ingredients to blender and blend until smooth.

2. Serve and enjoy!

Avocado-Berry Smoothie

This smoothie is sure to become a favorite.

Servings: 1

½ avocado, peeled, pitted, cubed

¼ cup coconut milk

½ cup fresh or frozen strawberries

½ cup frozen raspberries

Juice of ¼ a lime

1. Place all ingredients in a blender. Blend until smooth.

2. Serve in tall glass and enjoy!

Carrot, Cabbage, and Peach Smoothie

Servings: 2

½ cup grapes

½ cup frozen peaches, sliced

¼ cup cabbage, chopped

½ large carrot

1/8 cup ice cubes

1/8 cup of water

1. In a blender, combine all ingredients. Blend until smooth.

2. Enjoy!

Minty Spinach and Avocado Smoothie

This smoothie will charge your batteries for the whole day.

Servings: 2

1 ripe avocado, pulp

1 cup spinach leaves

½ cup mint leaves

2 cups coconut milk

1 frozen banana

1. Add all ingredients to blender and blend until smooth.

2. Transfer into serving glasses.

3. Enjoy!

Mango and Spinach Sunrise Smoothie

You will definitely enjoy this smoothie recipe.

Servings: 2

1 cup mango, cut into chunks

1 cup spinach

2 cups orange juice

1 banana

3 tablespoons lime juice

¼ teaspoon black pepper

1. Add all ingredients to blender and blend until smooth.

2. Transfer into serving glasses.

3. Enjoy!

Healthy Spinach and Pineapple Smoothie

This smoothie will give you extra energy for the whole day.

Servings: 2

1 cup pineapple slices

1 cup spinach leaves

2 cups coconut milk

1 frozen banana

1 tablespoon brown sugar

1. Add all ingredients to blender and blend until smooth.

2. Transfer into serving glasses.

3. Enjoy!

SALADS

Salads are a healthy choice for lunch or dinner.

Take one on the go by layering into a mason jar.

We've got choices here for all tastes.

Asian Noodle Mason Jar Salad

Healthy out-the-door lunch that's sure to please!

Servings: 4

1/4 cup rice wine vinegar

1/4 cup soy sauce (low-sodium)

1 teaspoon sesame oil

4 tablespoons extra-virgin olive oil

juice from 1 lime

1 large garlic clove, minced

1 tablespoon sugar

2 teaspoons red pepper flakes

1 cup carrots, shredded

2 celery stalks, diced

1 cup red cabbage, shredded

1/2 red bell pepper, diced

1 package soba noodles, cooked

1/1 cup fresh cilantro, minced

1/2 cup peanuts, roasted and unsalted

1. In a bowl, whisk together the rice wine vinegar, soy sauce, sesame oil, olive oil, lime juice, garlic, sugar, and red pepper flakes.

2. Divide this mixture evenly among the four mason jars.

3. Next, layer the remaining ingredients into the jars in this order: carrots, celery, cabbage, red pepper, soba noodles, cilantro, and peanuts.

4. Seal jars and refrigerate until ready to eat.

5. To serve, shake jar to coat salad with dressing.

6. Pour into bowl or eat right from the jar.

Marinated Tomato and Kale Salad

Superfoods kale and chia seeds team up in this delicious salad.

Servings: 1

½ bunch of leafy kale

½ tablespoon of sliced and toasted almonds

¼ cup chopped sundried tomatoes

½ tablespoon chia seeds

1 tablespoon olive oil

Squeeze of fresh lemon juice

Salt to taste

1. Wash and dry kale thoroughly.

2. Cut off the edges of the kale leaves and place into a bowl.

3. Mix in the olive oil, lemon juice, and salt into the same bowl as the kale.

4. Add in chia seeds, almonds, and chopped tomatoes. Add in your dressing, toss it, let it sit for 5 minutes, and then serve.

Kale and Orange Salad
with Cranberry Vinaigrette

Tasty and plentiful salad that is sure to fill you up!

Servings: 2

2 tablespoons extra-virgin olive oil

½ tablespoon maple syrup

1 tablespoon red wine vinegar

½ tablespoon cranberry juice

¼ cup fresh cranberries, rinsed, picked over, finely chopped

1 teaspoon fresh ginger, peeled, finely grated

1 cup kale leaves, trimmed, coarsely chopped

½ of a medium navel orange, peeled, sliced coarsely

Kosher salt and freshly ground black pepper, to taste

1. In a salad bowl, mix olive oil, maple syrup, vinegar, and cranberry juice until well blended. Stir in cranberries and ginger. Add a little salt and pepper.

2. Add in kale and orange slices, toss well to coat. Cover and chill for at least 15 minutes to an hour before serving.

Spinach Salad with Apple

Servings: 2

1 ½ tablespoons extra-virgin olive oil

1 tablespoon cider vinegar

½ tablespoon horseradish, prepared

¼ teaspoon sea salt

½ red apple, halved, cored, sliced

¼ cup pomegranate seeds

1/8 cup red onion, thinly sliced

¼ pound fresh baby spinach, rinsed, stems cut, leaves torn

1. In a salad bowl, combine oil, vinegar, and horseradish, whisk to blend. Season with salt, mix in apple, pomegranate seeds, and onion, toss to combine. Refrigerate for 30 minutes.

2. Add spinach, mix, and serve.

Wheat Berry, Apple, and Walnut Salad

Healthy, whole grain salad with lots of flavor!

Servings: 2

1 cup of wheat berries

4 cups of water

¼ cup extra-virgin olive oil

5 tablespoons lemon juice, divided

½ scallion, chopped

1/6 cup fresh parsley, chopped

Salt and pepper to taste

1 large apple, diced with skin

¼ cup celery, diced

¼ cup dried cherries

¼ cup walnuts, chopped and toasted

1. Combine water and wheat berries in a large pot. Bring to a boil, reduce heat, and cook wheat berries for 1 hour, or until tender. Drain and let cool.

2. In a bowl, whisk together olive oil, 4 tablespoons lemon juice, scallion, parsley, salt, and pepper.

3. Put apples in a small bowl and toss with remaining 1 tablespoon of lemon juice.

4. Add all ingredients to a large bowl and mix well to combine.

Mixed Vegetable and Fruit Salad

Servings: 2

½ apple, skin on, diced

½ cup cantaloupe, diced

¼ English cucumber, diced

½ orange, zested and flesh cut up, diced

½ lime, zested and juiced

Cinnamon

Sea salt and black pepper to taste

Fresh basil leaves, as garnish

1. In bowl, combine all ingredients. Mix to incorporate. Season with salt and pepper to taste.

2. Scoop into serving bowls, garnish with additional cinnamon and basil leaves.

Simple Cucumber and Onion Salad

Servings: 4

¼ cup vinegar

3 tablespoons olive oil

½ teaspoon salt

¼ teaspoon black pepper

1 cup cucumber, sliced

1 red onion, sliced

2 tablespoons fresh coriander, chopped

1. In a bowl whisk together olive oil, vinegar, black pepper, and salt.

2. Add cucumber, onion, and mix well.

3. Sprinkle coriander on top.

4. Serve and enjoy.

Strawberry Salad

Tasty and refreshing salad!

Servings: 1

½ pint strawberries, washed and cut

1 ½ cups baby greens

½ celery stalk, chopped

½ fennel bulb, chopped

1/8 cup balsamic vinegar

¼ cup extra-virgin olive oil

Freshly ground black pepper, to taste

1. Add strawberries, baby greens, celery, and fennel to salad bowl.

2. In a small bowl, whisk together vinegar, oil, and pepper. Pour dressing over salad. Toss to coat.

Black Bean and Corn Salad

Healthy salad that can be served as a side dish or as a meal!

Servings: 3

1 cup cooked black beans

Kernels from 1 ear of cooked corn (about 1 cup)

1.5 medium vine-ripened or heirloom tomatoes, diced

½ yellow bell pepper, diced

½ cucumber, peeled, seeded and diced

½ ripe avocado, diced

½ small onion, diced

1/8 cup fresh lime juice

1 1/2 tablespoons olive oil

1 clove of garlic, minced

½ large handful fresh basil, chopped

½ teaspoon salt

¼ teaspoon garlic powder

1/8 teaspoon black pepper

1. In a large bowl, combine beans, corn, tomato, bell pepper, cucumber, avocado, and onion.

2. In a small bowl, whisk together lime juice, olive oil, garlic, basil, salt, garlic powder, and black pepper.

3. Chill for 1 hour, taste and add extra lime juice and salt, as needed.

4. Serve cold.

Couscous Salad

Very healthy and easy lunch!

Servings: 1

1/3 cup water

1/3 cup of couscous (not cooked)

1 ½ teaspoons olive oil

 1 teaspoon lemon juice

Dash of salt

¼ cup cucumber, chopped

½ Roma tomato, chopped

1 tablespoon green onion, chopped

3-4 Kalamata olives, halved

1. Pour water into large microwave-safe mug and microwave for 3 minutes.

2. Add couscous to mug and cover with a plate or napkin. Let it sit for 5 minutes and then fluff with a fork.

3. Add the olive oil, lemon juice, and salt to mug and stir.

4. Add in cucumber, tomato, green onion, and olives. Stir.

5. Serve immediately, or refrigerate for one hour if you prefer a chilled couscous salad

Vegan "Chicken" Salad

Vegan twist on the versatile chicken salad!

Servings: 2

6 ounces tempeh, cubed

1 teaspoon of lemon juice

½ stalk of celery, diced

½ cup of any vegan mayonnaise of your choice

¼ cup minced green onions

½ teaspoon of mustard

Salt and pepper to taste

1. Bring pot of water to a boil. Add tempeh, reduce heat, and simmer for 15 minutes. Drain and let cool.

2. Combine tempeh, lemon juice, celery, and onions in a bowl.

3. Add in vegan mayonnaise and mustard. Stir.

4. Season with salt and pepper to taste

5. Chill in refrigerator and serve!

Simple White Bean Salad

Healthy and simple lunch or dinner!

Servings: 2

1 6 oz. can of white beans, rinsed and drained

¼ cup red onion, chopped

1 teaspoon lemon juice

1 teaspoon wine vinegar

½ tablespoon olive oil

½ teaspoon of rosemary

½ teaspoon thyme

Salt and pepper to taste

1. Combine white beans and onion in bowl, add lemon juice and let it marinate for about 15 minutes.

2. In small bowl, whisk together vinegar, olive oil, rosemary, thyme, salt, and pepper. Pour over bean mixture and mix.

3. Chill in refrigerator for 2-3 hours and serve.

Black Bean Mason Jar Salad

Quick out-the-door salad you can make ahead of time.

Servings: 1

1 diced green bell pepper

¼ cup corn kernels

4 chopped baby tomatoes

¼ cup cooked quinoa

¼ cup cooked black beans

¼ avocado

½ cup spinach

Dressing of your choice

1. In a mason jar, first add your dressing, then add peppers, corn, tomatoes, quinoa, beans, avocado, and spinach

2. Store in refrigerator and shake when ready to eat.

Mexican Salad

Very easy and affordable salad.

Servings: 6

1 cup chickpea, boiled

1 cup black beans, boiled

1 onion, chopped

2 tomatoes, chopped

½ teaspoon salt

1 teaspoon black pepper

2 garlic cloves, minced

4 tablespoons cilantro, chopped

3 tablespoons olive oil

1 jalapeno, chopped

1. In a bowl combine all ingredients and toss.

2. Freeze for 10 minutes before serving.

3. Serve and enjoy.

Refreshing Cucumber and Tomato Salad

Wonderful summertime, or anytime, salad.

Servings: 4

1 cup cucumber, chopped

1 onion, thinly sliced

2 tomatoes, chopped

2 garlic cloves, minced

1 tablespoon olive oil

4-5 black olives, sliced

¼ cup lime juice

Salt and freshly ground black pepper

1. In a bowl combine cucumber, onion, olive oil, tomatoes, garlic, olives, lime juice, and mix.

2. Season with salt and black pepper.

3. Serve and enjoy.

Sweet and Sour Fruit Salad

This dish is made with healthy fruits and seasoned with salt, red pepper, sugar, and lemon juice. Feel free to mix and match fruits depending on what you have on hand.

Servings: 4

1/2 cup bananas, cut into chunks

1/2 cup ripe apple, cut into chunks

1/2 cup mangoes, cut into chunks

1/2 cup strawberries, cut into chunks

1/2 cup cherries, cut into chunks

 1/2 cup oranges, peeled, cut into chunks

¼ teaspoon salt

1 tablespoon sugar

¼ teaspoon black pepper

½ teaspoon red chili powder

¼ cup lemon juice

1. In a bowl combine all fruits and mix thoroughly.

2. Season with salt, sugar, black pepper, chili powder, and toss.

3. Drizzle lemon juice and mix.

4. Serve and enjoy.

Raw Vegan Ranch Dressing

A simple, quick, flavorful, and nutritious recipe.

Servings: 8

3 tablespoons water

4 tablespoons vinegar

1 cup cashews, soaked

1 Hass avocado, slices

1 cup cucumber, chopped

½ cup spring onion, chopped

½ teaspoon salt

½ teaspoon black pepper

1 tablespoon olive oil

1 tablespoon parsley

1 teaspoon thyme

1. In a blender add water, vinegar, cashew, avocado, and blend until smooth.

2. Add cucumber, onion, salt, black pepper, olive oil, parsley, thyme, and blend again.

3. Can be stored for up to 1 week, covered in refrigerator.

Ginger Zest Tahini Dressing

Servings: 6

1 cup tahini

1 inch ginger slice

1 teaspoon sesame seeds

1 teaspoon mustard paste

2 tablespoons lemon juice

1 teaspoon salt

1 teaspoon black pepper

1. In a blender add all ingredients and blend until smooth.

2. Store in covered glass container in refrigerator.

SANDWICHES AND LIGHT MEALS

This section covers wraps, pizzas, soups, and sandwiches.

These are good for lunches or light dinners.

Hummus and Veggie Wrap

Quick and easy customizable wrap that you can make in minutes!

Servings: 1

1 whole wheat tortilla

2 tablespoon of hummus

½ of a ripe avocado

¼ cup of red bell peppers

1/8 cup of baby tomatoes

Any other veggies of your choice!

1. Spread hummus on tortilla.

2. Add avocado and rest of assorted veggies.

3. Wrap up the tortilla, slice in half, and enjoy!

Pineapple Microwave Pizzas

Classic English muffin pizzas with a vegan twist!

Servings: 1

1 English muffin

¼ cup of pizza sauce

1 cup of shredded vegan mozzarella

¼ cup of pineapple, sliced

1. Slice English muffin and toast both sides.

2. Add half of pizza sauce on each muffin.

3. Top with cheese and pineapple slices.

4. Put on plate and microwave for 45 seconds.

5. Serve and enjoy!

Shitake Soup with Squash and Mustard Greens

Servings: 3-4

7 dried shiitake mushrooms, soaked in boiling water

6 cups vegetable stock

¼ small butternut squash, peeled, seeded, cubed

1 ½ tablespoons soy sauce

½ red onion, quartered and sliced in thin rings

1 large garlic clove, finely chopped

½ large rosemary sprig

2 large mustard greens, stems removed and coarsely chopped

1. Place dried shiitake mushrooms in bowl and add 1 cup boiling water. Let soak for 15 minutes.

2. In a large pot, bring broth to boil over high heat. Add in squash, lower heat, cover and simmer about 10 minutes.

3. While squash is cooking, remove mushrooms from bowl (reserve liquid). Trim mushrooms and cut in strips. Add mushrooms and reserved liquid to pot with squash.

4. Add soy sauce, red onion, garlic, and rosemary. Continue simmering until squash is tender, about 5-6 minutes.

5. Stir in chopped greens and allow several seconds to wilt and turn bright green. Pull pan off heat and serve in bowls at once.

Purple Sweet Potato Soup

Servings: 2

½ tablespoon olive oil

¼ onion, chopped

¾ pound purple sweet potato, peeled, chopped

2 cups vegetable broth

1/8 cup coconut milk

Sea salt and freshly ground black pepper, to taste

1. In a saucepan, heat oil over medium-high heat. Add onion and cook for about 5 minutes or until just softened. Add sweet potatoes and broth, cover, and bring to boil. Reduce heat and simmer for about 30 minutes or until potatoes are tender.

2. Transfer into a blender and mix until pureed. Transfer back into the pot, add coconut milk and heat until heated through. Season with salt and pepper. Serve hot.

Peanut Butter Apple Pinwheels

Servings: 1

½ thinly sliced apple

2 tablespoons peanut butter

1 large flour tortilla

1/8 cup raisins

toothpicks

1. Place tortilla on a flat surface and spread the peanut butter evenly on top.

2. Distribute the apple slices and raisins evenly on top.

3. Roll up the tortilla tightly and slice into 1 inch pieces.

4. Secure each piece with a toothpick and enjoy!

Mini Microwave Pizzas

Whip these up for an almost-instant snack.

Servings: 1

1 English muffin

¼ cup of pizza sauce

1 cup of shredded vegan mozzarella

Assorted veggies

1. Slice English muffin and toast both sides.

2. Add half of pizza sauce on each muffin.

3. Top with cheese and the veggies of your choice.

4. Put on plate and microwave for 45 seconds.

Chips and Salsa Avocado Toast

Yummy snack or breakfast that only takes 5 minutes!

Servings: 1

1 slice of whole grain bread

½ of an avocado, mashed

1 tablespoon of salsa

1 teaspoon of crushed tortilla chips

1. Toast slice of whole grain toast and top with mashed avocado.

2. Spoon on one tablespoon of salsa and add crushed chips on top.

3. Serve and enjoy!

Open-Faced Tomato Pesto Melted Sandwich

This easy and delicious sandwich is seriously good.

Servings: 2

2 thick-cut slices of crusty bread

¼ cup pesto

4 slices of tomato

1 teaspoon olive oil

Salt and freshly ground black pepper, to taste

½ teaspoon dried basil or 1 tablespoon chopped fresh basil

1. Preheat oven or toaster oven to 400 degrees F.

2. Place bread slices on baking sheet.

3. Spread pesto in thick layer on each slice of bread. Top with 2 tomato slices on each slice. Drizzle with olive oil and season with salt, pepper, and basil.

4. Bake in oven for about 10 minutes, until tomatoes soften and bread gets crispy.

5. For crispier bread, place under broiler for several minutes, watching closely to prevent burning.

6. Remove from oven and enjoy!

Veggie Black Bean Burritos

So good, these are great for lunch or dinner.

Servings: 2

2 (10-inch) flour tortillas

2 tablespoons olive oil

1 small onion, chopped

½ red bell pepper, chopped

1 clove garlic, minced

1 teaspoon jalapeno peppers

1 (15 ounce) can black beans, rinsed and drained

Salt and freshly ground black pepper, to taste

2 tablespoons fresh cilantro, chopped

Additional toppings: salsa, guacamole, lettuce, red onions

1. Wrap tortillas in foil and place in 300-degree F oven for 10-15 minutes.

2. While tortillas are warming, heat oil in skillet over medium-high heat. Add onions, bell pepper, garlic, and jalapeno and sauté for 2-3 minutes. Add black beans and continue to cook for 3-4 minutes, stirring occasionally.

3. Season with salt and pepper and stir in cilantro. Remove from heat.

4. To assemble, spoon half of bean mixture down center of each tortilla. Top with additional toppings of your choice. Roll tortillas up and serve.

BLT plus Avocado Pita Pockets

So easy, yet so delicious!

Servings: 1

2 slices bread of your choice

Vegan mayo

Tomato slices

Lettuce leaves

Vegan bacon, cooked (MorningStar Farms or similar)

Avocado slices

Salt and freshly ground black pepper

1. Toast bread and then spread a layer of mayo on each slice.

2. Layer one slice with tomato slices, lettuce, vegan bacon, and avocado. Season with salt and pepper.

3. Top with remaining slice of bread. Cut and serve.

Tofu Burgers

So delicious, make up a batch and have a go-to lunch all week. These freeze well too.

Servings: 6 burgers

1 pound firm tofu, drained

½ cup bread crumbs

¼ cup whole wheat flour

1 tablespoon Dijon mustard

1 ½ tablespoons soy sauce

1 teaspoon cumin

½ teaspoon cayenne

½ teaspoon garlic powder

½ teaspoon onion salt

1 tablespoon olive oil

1. Mash tofu with fork in large bowl. Add in all other ingredients except for olive oil and mix well.

2. Form into 6 patties. Place on plate and chill in refrigerator for about 30 minutes.

3. Heat oil in large skillet over medium-high heat. Add burgers and cook until golden brown, 4-5 minutes. Flip over and cook until golden brown on other side.

4. Serve hot, on hamburger buns or toasted bread with your choice of toppings.

Spicy Chickpea Wraps

Inspired by Indian cuisine, these wraps will keep you satisfied all afternoon long.

Servings: 4

1 tablespoon olive oil

1 small onion, chopped

2 garlic cloves, minced

1 teaspoon curry powder

½ teaspoon ginger

½ teaspoon cumin

¼ teaspoon coriander

¼ teaspoon cayenne pepper

1 can (15 ounces) chickpeas, rinsed and drained

1 can (15 ounces) chopped tomatoes

2 cups baby spinach

4 tortillas (10 inch)

1. Heat olive oil in large skillet over medium-high heat. Add onion and sauté for 2-3 minutes. Add garlic and sauté another minute. Add in seasonings and stir. Add chickpeas and chopped tomatoes, reduce heat to medium, and cook, stirring occasionally for 5 minutes.

2. While chickpeas are cooking, wrap tortillas in foil and place in 350 degree F oven to warm.

3. To assemble, spread chickpea mixture in center of tortilla, top with spinach, roll up, and serve.

Stuffed Sweet Potatoes

These black-bean stuffed sweet potatoes are insanely good.

Servings: 2

2 medium-large sweet potatoes

1 teaspoon olive oil

1 small onion, chopped

2 cloves garlic, minced

½ red bell pepper, chopped

1 can (15 ounces) black beans

½ cup tomato sauce

1 tablespoon chili powder

1 teaspoon cumin

½ teaspoon cayenne pepper, optional

1 teaspoon oregano

½ teaspoon salt

Freshly ground black pepper, to taste

¼ cup vegan cheese, shredded

Guacamole, for topping

1. Preheat oven to 400 degrees F. Poke a couple of holes in sweet potatoes with fork and then wrap in aluminum foil. Bake in oven for 45 minutes or until tender.

2. Meanwhile, prepare topping. Heat olive oil in skillet over medium-high heat. Add onion and sauté for 2-3 minutes. Add garlic and bell pepper and sauté for another 2-3 minutes until softened.

3. Add undrained beans, tomato sauce, and seasonings. Stir to blend. Allow to simmer on low heat, stirring occasionally, while sweet potatoes are baking.

4. When sweet potatoes are done, remove from oven, unwrap, and cut down the middle. Top with generous portion of black bean mixture, sprinkling of vegan cheese, and spoonful of guacamole. Serve immediately.

Vegan "Tuna" Salad

This faux tuna salad is very easy to make and just as satisfying as the real thing.

Servings: 4

- **1 can (15 ounces) chickpeas, rinsed and drained**
- **1/3 cup vegan mayo**
- **½ tablespoon Dijon mustard**
- **1 celery stalk, chopped**
- **¼ red onion, chopped**
- **¼ cup sweet pickles, diced**
- **1 tablespoon capers, optional**
- **¼ teaspoon cayenne pepper**
- **Salt and freshly ground black pepper, to taste**

1. Add chickpeas to bowl and mash with fork. Add vegan mayo, Dijon mustard, celery, onion, pickles, capers, cayenne pepper, salt, and pepper. Mix well to combine.
2. Serve on toasted bread topped with lettuce, tomato, and additional mayo.

Lentil Cakes

These lentil burgers are yummy with lettuce, tomato, and ketchup

on a sesame seed bun.

Servings: 8

1 cup dried lentils

2 ½ cups water

¼ cup almond milk

½ cup oats

1 envelope onion soup mix

½ cup chopped walnuts

¾ cup bread crumbs

Salt and freshly ground black pepper

1 tablespoon soy sauce

2 tablespoons olive oil

1. Add lentils and water to saucepan and bring to boil. Reduce heat to low, cover, and cook until tender, about 40 minutes. Remove from heat and drain.

2. Add lentils to large mixing bowl and add almond milk, oats, onion soup mix, walnuts, bread crumbs, salt, pepper, and soy sauce. Mix together until well blended. Form into 8 patties.

3. Heat olive oil in skillet over medium-high heat. Fry patties, in batches, for 2-3 minutes per side.

Yummy Ramen Noodles

Quick, cheap, and loaded with veggies, these noodles make an easy lunch.

Pack them in a mason jar and take them on the go.

Servings:1

1 scallion, chopped

¼ cup sliced mushrooms

¼ broccoli, cut into small pieces

3-4 baby carrots, sliced thin

¼ cup green peas

1 package vegan ramen noodles

1 tablespoon soy sauce

1 tablespoon sesame oil

Salt and freshly ground black pepper, to taste

1. Bring 2 cups water to boil in saucepan. Add scallion, mushrooms, broccoli, carrots, and peas. Lower heat to medium and cook for 2-3 minutes.

2. Add noodles, soy sauce, sesame oil, salt, and pepper. Stir and cook for 1 minute. Remove from heat. Adjust seasonings to taste.

3. Pour into bowl and serve hot.

Note: To make an on-the-go lunch, combine all ingredients in mason jar. When ready to eat, add boiling water to cover. Allow to sit for several minutes. Stir and enjoy.

SNACKS AND DIPS

When you're hungry between meals, reach for one of these tasty,

satisfying, and healthy snacks. Great for when friends

come over to hang out, too.

Tomato Bruschetta

Ready in under 5 minutes.

Servings: 2

½ loaf French bread

1 large tomato, chopped

1/2 onion, chopped

¼ cup pineapple, chunks

¼ teaspoon salt

¼ cup mango, chunks

1 ½ tablespoons lemon juice

¼ teaspoon black pepper

¼ teaspoon oregano

1 teaspoon olive oil

¼ teaspoon garlic powder

1. Cut French bread into 6 equal parts. Place preheated 350 degree F oven or toaster oven and toast until lightly browned, 2-3 minutes.

2. Place all remaining ingredients in bowl and toss to combine.

3. Top each bread slice with tomato mixture and transfer into serving dish.

4. Serve and enjoy.

Homemade Guacamole

Healthy, versatile dip for all occasions.

Servings: 3-4

2 avocados

½ of a lime

½ of salt

¼ cup of diced onion

1 plum tomato, chopped small

½ teaspoon minced garlic

2 tablespoon chopped cilantro

1. In a medium sized bowl, mash avocados, salt, and lime juice together.

2. Add in cilantro, garlic, onion, and tomatoes.

3. Refrigerate for 1 hour before serving.

Curried Zucchini Chips

Servings: 2

1 medium zucchini, thinly sliced

1 tablespoon olive oil

¼ teaspoon curry powder

1/8 teaspoon garlic powder

1/8 teaspoon salt

1. Lightly grease paper-lined baking sheet.

2. Arrange zucchini slices in a single layer on the prepared baking sheet. Drizzle olive oil and sprinkle with curry powder, garlic powder, and salt.

3. Place baking sheet in oven and bake at 350 degrees F for 12 minutes. Flip zucchini over and cook for an additional 10 minutes or until very crisp. Cool and store in an airtight container.

Sweet and Spiced Nuts

Great party snack or appetizer!

Servings: 6

½ cup walnuts, halved

½ cup pecan halves

½ cup cashews

½ cup almonds

1 ½ tablespoons melted vegan butter

¼ cup sugar

1/8 cup water

¼ teaspoon cumin

¼ teaspoon cayenne pepper

½ teaspoon salt

¼ teaspoon ground pepper

1. Combine walnuts, pecans, cashews, and almonds in a large bowl.

2. In a small bowl add melted vegan butter, sugar, water, cumin, cayenne pepper, salt, and pepper. Pour the mixture over nuts. Stir to coat nuts thoroughly.

3. Spread nuts in a pan. Cook at 350 degrees F for 10 minutes. Stir and cook for an additional 3-4 minutes.

Tangy Avocado Hummus with Rosemary

½ avocado, peeled and pitted

1 cup canned chickpeas, rinsed and drained

1/8 cup sesame seeds

½ lime, zested and juiced

1/8 cup water

1 tablespoon olive oil

1 tablespoon fresh rosemary, chopped

1. In a food processor or blender, combine all ingredients; blend until smooth.

2. Serve in bowls with pita bread or veggies!

Rosemary and Olive Oil Popcorn

Healthy and quick alternative to the boxed stuff!

Servings: 2

¼ cup popcorn seeds

½ tablespoon of fresh rosemary, finely chopped

1 tablespoon olive oil

Salt to taste

1. Place popcorn seeds in a brown bag and seal tightly by folding top.

2. Microwave on high for 2 minutes or until popping stops.

3. Place popcorn in a bowl and drizzle with olive oil.

4. Add rosemary and salt and enjoy!

Chopped Turnip Appetizer

Great, healthy appetizer all your friends will love!

Servings: 5

½ rutabaga, peeled and chopped

½ turnip, peeled and chopped

1/8 cup olive oil

½ small onion, chopped

½ clove of garlic, minced

Black pepper to taste

1. In a food processor set at high, process rutabaga and turnip, adding olive oil while mixing, until smooth.

2. Combine garlic and onions, process for about 4 minutes or until very smooth. Add more oil to desired consistency. Season with pepper to taste.

Beet Chips

A delicious way to eat your veggies.

Servings: 2

2 beets

1 teaspoon olive oil

Salt to taste

1. Preheat oven to 350 degrees F.

2. Peel beets and slice into thin slices.

3. Place beets in bowl and add olive oil and salt. Mix to coat.

4. Spread beets in single layer on baking sheet. Bake for 30-35 minutes, until edges start to dry out and beets turn lighter in color.

5. Cool on wire racks. Eat at once or store in airtight container.

Cherry-Chocolate Chip Granola Bars

Packed with nutrients these granola bars are a perfect snack to keep you energized all afternoon.

Servings: 12 bars

2 ½ cups rolled oats

½ cup all-purpose flour

½ cup maple syrup

¾ cup vegan chocolate chips

½ cup dried cherries

1/3 cup applesauce

¼ cup sunflower seeds

½ cup sliced almonds

½ cup coconut chips

½ teaspoon cinnamon

½ teaspoon vanilla extract

1. Preheat oven to 350 degrees F. Spray 7 x 11 ½ inch pan with nonstick cooking spray.

2. In large bowl, mix together all ingredients. Lightly press into pan.

3. Bake for 20 minutes or until golden brown. Allow to cool before cutting.

Vegan Nachos

Even your non-vegan friends are going to love these nachos.

Servings: 4

For the Cheese Sauce:

¼ cup all-purpose flour

¼ cup nutritional yeast

1 teaspoon salt

¼ teaspoon garlic powder

1 teaspoon paprika

¼ teaspoon ground cumin

1 cup water

2 tablespoons vegan butter

1 can (10 ounces) diced tomatoes and green chilies (Ro*tel)

4 cups tortilla chips

1 tomato diced

1 cup vegan refried beans

½ cup corn kernels

1 avocado, peeled, seeded, and diced

1. Preheat oven to 350 degrees F. Spray baking dish with nonstick cooking spray.

2. In saucepan, combine flour, nutritional yeast, salt, garlic powder, paprika, cumin, and water over medium-heat. Stir continuously until mixture thickens and bubbles, about 5 minutes. Stir in vegan butter and stir until melted, about 1 minute. Stir in diced tomatoes and chilies, turn heat to low, and simmer, stirring occasionally, for 4-5 minutes. Remove from heat.

3. Spread tortilla chips in baking dish. Pour cheese sauce over chips. Top with tomatoes, refried beans, corn kernels, and avocado.

4. Place in oven and bake for 10 minutes. Serve immediately.

Trail Mix

A mixture of dried fruit, nuts, and seeds makes this trail mix a go-to energy snack.

Servings: 8

½ cup dried apricots

½ dried apples

½ raisins (or dried cranberries)

1 cup sunflower seeds, unsalted

½ cup dry-roasted peanuts, unsalted

½ cup almonds, unsalted

½ cup pretzel twists

¼ cup vegan mini chocolate chips

1. Mix together all ingredients in bowl. Place into portion size containers to store.

Microwavable Kale Chips

Quick and homemade kale chips you can make in the microwave!

Servings: 2

¼ bunch of kale

2 tablespoon of olive oil

Salt to taste

1. Remove the stems from the kale, rip leaves into 2 inch pieces, and thoroughly wash and dry.

2. Spread all leaves on a large plate and drizzle with olive oil.

3. Microwave for 2 minutes or until crispy.

4. Toss into a bowl and enjoy!

Seasoned Chili Popcorn

Servings: 2

½ cup popcorn seeds

2 tablespoons vegetable oil

2 tablespoons of vegan butter, melted (Earth Balance or similar)

Salt to taste

Chili powder

1. In a brown paper bag add, popcorn seeds and salt. Secure the top by folding and microwave for 2-3 minutes or until popping slows.

2. Drizzle with oil and butter, sprinkle with salt and chili powder. Mix to combine.

Roasted Chickpeas

Healthy and yummy snack everyone will enjoy!

Servings: 2

1 (12 ounce) can chickpeas, rinsed and drained

2 tablespoons olive oil

Salt to taste

1. Heat oven to 425 degrees F.

2. Place chickpeas in a bowl and drizzle on olive oil, salt, and any other seasonings you would like. Mix to coat.

3. Spread chickpeas in single layer on baking sheet. Bake for 30-35 until chickpeas are browned, turning once during cooking.

4. That's it, enjoy!

Homemade Hummus

Healthy, quick, and homemade version of the classic hummus.

Servings: Makes about 1.5 cups

1 mashed garlic clove

1 (15 ounce) can chickpeas, rinsed and drained

1/3 cup of roasted tahini

1/8 cup of lemon juice

¼ cup of water

1/8 cup olive oil

¼ teaspoon of salt

Parsley (optional for garnish)

1. Add all ingredients except salt and parsley in a food processor or blender and process until smooth

2. Add in salt to taste.

3. Spoon out into a bowl, garnish with parsley, and serve with crackers, pita bread, or veggies!

Artichoke and Spinach Dip

This healthy dip is made with spinach, artichoke, cashews, jalapeno, and mustard paste.

Servings: 6

1 cup spinach leaves

3 artichokes, peeled, chopped

6-7 black olives

1 cup cashews

1 tablespoon olive oil

1 teaspoon salt

1 teaspoon mustard paste

½ teaspoon jalapeno, seeded, chopped

1. Add all ingredients to blender and blend until smooth.

2. Enjoy!

Ginger Energy Bites

Quick and easy snack for those times when you need a burst of energy.

Servings: 4

1 cup of raw almonds

1 cup of pitted dates

1 cup of cashews

1 ½ inch piece of fresh ginger

Salt to taste

1. Add all ingredients to food processor or blender and blend until it starts to crumbly.

2. Roll mixture into teaspoon-sized balls and refrigerate for 1 hour before serving.

Mango and Avocado Salsa

A wonderful combination of mango and avocado.

Servings: 4

1 cup mango, cut into chunks

1 avocado, peeled, pitted, and cut into cubes

1 teaspoon fresh cilantro, chopped

2 tablespoons lemon juice

½ teaspoon salt ½ teaspoon black pepper

¼ teaspoon chili powder

1 teaspoon parsley, chopped

1. In a large bowl add mango chunks, avocado, cilantro, and lemon juice. Toss to combine.

2. Season with salt, black pepper, and chili powder.

3. Sprinkle parsley on top and serve.

4. Enjoy!

MAIN DISHES

Cooking a healthy, delicious, vegan main dish does not have to be difficult or expensive. This chapter contains a variety of great recipes that will inspire you to cook dinner for yourself and your friends!

Indian Beans and Rice

Healthy and tasty dinner that you can make in the microwave!

Servings: 1

1/2 cup canned small red beans, rinsed and drained

2 tablespoons finely chopped red onions

2 tablespoons finely chopped red bell peppers

2 teaspoons finely chopped cilantro

1 teaspoon fresh lime juice

1 teaspoon tomato paste

½ teaspoon sugar

Dash of salt

1/2 cup cooked rice

1. In a large microwave-safe mug add the beans, onions, bell pepper, cilantro, lime juice, tomato paste, sugar, and salt.

2. Microwave for about 2 minutes, or until hot. Stir.

3. Serve on top of rice and enjoy!

Rice, Edamame, and Pineapple in a Mug

Filling dinner or lunch that can be made in a mug!

Servings: 1

½ cup brown rice

⅔ water

⅓ cup shelled edamame

¼ cup pineapple

1 tablespoon teriyaki sauce

2 tablespoons finely chopped cashews

Cilantro for garnish (optional)

1. In a large microwave-safe mug, add in the rice and water and put edamame on top.

2. Cover mug with a plate or napkin and microwave for 5-6 minutes.

3. Let stand for 1 minute.

4. Stir in the pineapple and teriyaki sauce and microwave again for 30 seconds.

5. Let it stand for 30 more seconds and then add in cashews. Garnish with cilantro.

6. Enjoy!

Microwaveable Vegan Macaroni and Cheese

Quick vegan comfort food you can make in the microwave!

Servings: 1

1/2 cup of uncooked macaroni noodles

1/2 cup of soy cheese alternative

¼ cup of almond milk (or soy milk)

¼ teaspoon of paprika

1 pinch of mustard powder

1 tablespoon of nutritional yeast

1. Boil macaroni according to box directions.

2. Drain pasta and place it into a microwaveable bowl.

3. Add in soy cheese and mix into pasta.

4. Pour milk and nutritional yeast into bowl and add paprika and mustard powder. Stir.

5. Microwave for about 1-2 minutes, or until cheese has melted.

6. Mix again and put back in microwave for another 30 seconds.

7. Serve!

Burrito in a Bowl

Super simple dinner or lunch!

Servings: 2

1 teaspoon olive oil

1 clove garlic, minced

½ diced red pepper

1/2 can (15 ounces) black beans, rinsed and drained

¼ cup water

½ cup frozen corn kernels

½ teaspoon cumin

½ teaspoon chili powder

1 cup brown rice, cooked

½ avocado, diced

1 tablespoon lime juice

Additional toppings: Salsa, shredded vegan cheese, chopped cilantro, diced red onion, tortilla chips

1. Heat olive oil in skillet over medium-high heat. Add garlic and red pepper and sauté for 2-3 minutes, until softened. Add black beans, water, corn kernels, cumin, and chili powder. Cook for another 4-5 minutes, stirring occasionally. Remove from heat.

2. Divide rice between two bowls. Add half of bean mixture to each bowl. Top with diced avocado and sprinkle with lime juice. Top with additional toppings of your choice.

Roasted Spaghetti Squash with Kale

Interesting take on classic spaghetti!

Servings: 2

½ whole spaghetti squash, seeded, halved

3 tablespoons olive oil, divided

Salt and black pepper, to taste

¼ whole onion, diced

1 bunch of kale, stalks removed and torn into pieces

½ teaspoon balsamic vinegar

1. Preheat oven to 350 degrees F.

2. Place spaghetti squash on a baking sheet, skin side down. Drizzle with 1 tablespoon olive oil on cut side and bake about an hour, until just fork tender.

3. Meanwhile, heat 1 tablespoon oil in skillet over medium-high heat. Sauté onions for about 3 minutes, or until tender. Mix in kale, sprinkle with salt and pepper, and cook for another 5 minutes or until kale is partly cooked. Remove from heat and set aside.

4. Shred the cooked squash using a fork and put into a bowl. Mix balsamic vinegar with remaining 1 tablespoon olive oil and drizzle over the shredded squash. Add salt and pepper; toss to blend.

5. Place spaghetti squash in serving bowls and top with sautéed kale and onion mixture.

Pesto Pasta Dish

Ten-minute super simple alfredo pesto pasta!

Servings: 1

4 oz. pasta of your choice

2 tablespoons pesto

1/8 cup almond milk

1 tablespoon of nutritional yeast

Handful of arugula

1 tablespoon of pine nuts, toasted

1. Cook pasta according to box instructions.

2. Add all ingredients into pasta and let it sit on the warm burner for 1 minute while stirring.

3. Enjoy!

Microwave Risotto Cup

A quick vegan risotto cup you can make in the microwave!

Servings: 1

½ tablespoon of vegan butter (Earth Balance or similar)

¼ onion, finely chopped

½ clove garlic, finely chopped

¼ cup of Arborio rice

½ cup of vegetable broth

1-2 tablespoon of white wine

1. To microwave-safe bowl, add butter and onions.

2. Microwave for 1 ½ minutes, stirring after 30 seconds.

3. Add garlic, rice, and broth to bowl and cover it loosely with plastic wrap. Microwave for 2 minutes.

4. Remove and stir. Add additional broth and repeat heating process if needed until rice reaches desired consistency.

Vegetable Microwave Curry

Healthy and filling dinner you can make in the microwave!

Servings: 2

½ sliced onion

1 1/2 cups of sliced veggies of your choice (cauliflower, broccoli, carrots)

1 can (15 ounces) chickpeas, rinsed and drained

1 ½ teaspoon curry powder

½ cup of coconut milk

½ tablespoon lemon juice

½ tablespoon soy sauce

¼ cup chopped nuts

1. Place onion, veggies, and chickpeas in microwave-safe casserole dish.

2. Cover and microwave for 2 minutes.

3. Add curry powder, coconut milk, soy sauce, and lemon juice. Stir to combine.

4. Microwave for another 5-6 minutes until vegetables are tender. Stir and check every 90 seconds.

5. Top with chopped nuts. Enjoy!

Fried Tofu with Tangy Peanut Sauce

Healthy and interesting vegan dinner!

Servings: 2

Ingredients for Tofu:

> 6 oz. firm tofu, drained, pressed, and cubed
>
> 2 tablespoon cornstarch
>
> Salt and black pepper to taste
>
> 3 tablespoon olive oil, for frying

Ingredients for Sauce:

> 3 tablespoon coconut milk
>
> 1 tablespoon peanut butter
>
> 1 teaspoon garlic powder
>
> 1 dash chili flakes
>
> 1 tablespoon ketchup
>
> 1 teaspoon lime juice
>
> Salt and black pepper to taste

1. In a bowl, place tofu and sprinkle cornstarch, toss to coat. Season it with salt and pepper.

2. In a skillet, heat oil over medium heat and cook tofu in batches until light brown on all sides.

3. Drain on paper towels to remove excess oil. Set aside while you prepare sauce.

4. In saucepan, heat coconut milk over medium heat. Stir in peanut butter. Add all other ingredients. Stir until smooth and heated through.

5. Pour sauce over tofu. Serve hot.

Pad Thai

Servings: 4

8 ounces rice noodles

2 tablespoons peanut oil

1 block tofu, extra-firm, blotted and diced

3 scallions, thinly sliced

2 cloves garlic, minced

1 large carrot, julienned

1 tomato, diced

4 tablespoons soy sauce

3 tablespoons brown sugar

1 teaspoon chili paste

2 cups bean sprouts

½ cup peanuts, crushed

2 tablespoon rice vinegar

Salt and freshly ground black pepper, to taste

Lime wedges, for garnish

1. Cook rice noodles according to package directions.

2. Heat oil in large skillet over medium-high heat. Add tofu and sauté until lightly browned, 3-4 minutes. Remove from pan and set aside.

3. In same pan, add scallions, garlic, carrots, and tomato. Sauté for 3-4 minutes. Add soy sauce, brown sugar, and chili paste. Stir to combine.

4. Add bean sprouts, rice noodles and tofu to pan and stir fry for 3-4 minutes. Add peanuts, rice vinegar, salt, and pepper. Stir for another minute.

5. Serve hot with lime wedges.

Vegetable Fried Rice

This dish is perfect for using up any leftover vegetables you may have. Feel free to experiment with whatever you have on hand.

Servings: 2

2 tablespoons oil (peanut or coconut work well)

3 cloves garlic, minced

4 scallions, sliced thinly

½ cup carrots, shredded or julienne

½ cup peas

½ cup broccoli florets, cut into small pieces

2 cups cooked brown or white rice

3 tablespoons soy sauce

1 teaspoon ground ginger

1 teaspoon chili sauce

Freshly ground black pepper, to taste

1. Heat oil in large skillet over medium-high heat. Add garlic, scallion, carrots, and broccoli and stir fry until vegetables are tender, about 5 minutes.

2. Add rice, soy sauce, ginger, chili sauce, and pepper. Stir fry for 3-4 more minutes.

3. Serve immediately with additional soy sauce, if desired.

Vegetarian Paella

This Spanish-style rice dish is sure to please.

Servings: 4

2 tablespoons olive oil

1 yellow onion, chopped

2 cloves garlic, minced

1 green bell pepper, chopped

1 red bell pepper, chopped

1 cup green beans, trimmed and cut in half

1 can (14 ounces) diced tomatoes

1 tablespoon paprika

1 bay leaf

1/2 teaspoon salt

1 teaspoon turmeric

1 cup Arborio rice

2 cups vegetable broth

1 cup green peas

1 jar (8 ounces) artichoke hearts, drained and quartered

1. Heat olive oil in large skillet over medium-high heat. Add onion, garlic, and peppers and cook, stirring, until onion softens and turns translucent and peppers are tender, about 5 minutes. Add garlic and sauté for another minute. Add green beans, tomatoes, paprika, bay leaf, salt, and turmeric and cook, stirring frequently, for another 3-4 minutes.

2. Add rice and vegetable broth and stir. Bring to boil, reduce heat to low and simmer, uncovered, for 15 minutes, stirring occasionally. Add additional broth/water if needed.

3. Add peas and artichoke hearts, cover pan, and cook for another 10 minutes, until remaining liquid is absorbed. Serve hot.

Stir Fry with Noodles

This colorful stir makes a quick and healthy dinner.

Servings: 3

8 ounces Udon noodles

2 tablespoons oil (peanut or coconut or safflower)

1 cup purple cabbage, shredded

1 red bell pepper, diced

1 large carrot, julienned or shredded

½ yellow onion, chopped

¼ cup soy sauce

1 teaspoon ground ginger

1 tablespoon sriracha

1. Cook Udon noodles according to package directions.

2. While noodles are cooking, heat oil in large skillet or wok over medium-high heat. Add cabbage, bell pepper, carrot, and onion and stir fry for 4-5 minutes. Add soy sauce, ginger, and sriracha and stir fry for 3-4 more minutes.

3. Add noodles and cook, stirring, for another 2-3 minutes. Add additional soy sauce if desired.

4. Serve hot.

Soft-Shell Tacos

Who doesn't love taco night?

Servings: 4

1 tablespoon olive oil

1 small onion, diced

2 cloves garlic, minced

½ bell pepper, diced

1 can (14.5 ounces) black beans, drained, rinsed

1 tablespoon cumin

1 teaspoon paprika

½ teaspoon cayenne pepper

½ teaspoon chili powder

½ cup salsa

4 corn tortillas, warmed

Optional toppings: Shredded lettuce, diced tomatoes, fresh cilantro

1. Heat oil in large skillet over medium heat. Add onions, garlic, and bell pepper; cook, stirring occasionally, for 4-5 minutes until vegetables are tender. Add beans and press down with spatula or wooden spoon to slightly smash beans. Stir in cumin, paprika, cayenne pepper, chili powder, and salsa. Lower heat, cover, and let simmer for 5 minutes.

2. To assemble taco, spread bean mixture in center of tortilla, top with additional salsa, shredded lettuce, diced tomatoes, and fresh cilantro.

Pho Noodle Soup

This traditional Vietnamese soup will warm you up on a chilly day.

Servings: 4

4 cups vegetable broth

1 teaspoon sriracha hot sauce

2 teaspoons fresh ginger, or 1 teaspoon dried ginger

2 tablespoon soy sauce

1 bay leaf

½ teaspoon salt

½ teaspoon black pepper

4 ounces extra-firm tofu, cubed

½ cup broccoli florets

½ cup sliced mushrooms

½ cup carrots, chopped

2 scallions, chopped

8 ounces rice noodles, cooked according to package directions

1. In large pot, combine vegetable broth, hot sauce, ginger, soy sauce, bay leaf, salt, and black pepper. Bring to boil. Add tofu, broccoli, mushrooms, carrots, and scallions. Reduce heat and simmer until vegetables are tender, about 5 minutes.

2. Divide noodles between four bowls. Ladle broth and vegetables over noodles. Serve hot.

Bean and Sweet Potato Chili

Whip up a batch of this sweet potato chili for a hearty dinner.

Enjoy the leftovers for lunch.

Servings: 3

½ tablespoon olive oil

½ yellow onion, chopped

1 clove garlic, minced

1 sweet potato, peeled and diced

1 tablespoon chili powder

½ tablespoon ground cumin

½ teaspoon paprika

½ teaspoon dried oregano

1 cup vegetable broth

½ tablespoon tomato paste

2 cups crushed tomatoes

1 can (15.5 ounces) kidney beans, rinsed and drained

1. Heat olive oil in large skillet over medium-high heat. Add onions and garlic and cook, stirring, until onions are translucent, about 5 minutes. Add sweet potatoes, chili powder, cumin, paprika, oregano, and vegetable broth. Stir in tomato paste. Simmer until sweet potatoes are tender, about 20 minutes.

2. Add crush tomatoes and beans. Let simmer, stirring occasionally, for 25 to 30 minutes. Serve hot.

Linguini with Avocado-Pesto Cream Sauce

This creamy sauce comes together quickly and easily.

Servings: 2

8 ounces dry linguini

1 ripe avocado, peeled, halved, and pitted

4 tablespoons pesto

1 clove garlic, minced

½ teaspoon paprika

Juice from ½ lemon

Salt and freshly ground black pepper, to taste

1. Cook linguini according to package directions.

2. While linguini is cooking, mash avocado in bowl. Stir in pesto, garlic, paprika, lemon juice, salt, and pepper. Mix until smooth.

3. When linguini is cooked, drain, reserving ¼ cup of the water.

4. Pour sauce over linguini and toss to coat. Add reserved water as needed to thin out the sauce. Serve hot.

Pasta Bows with Spinach and Chickpeas

Servings: 4

10 ounces pasta bows

1 tablespoon olive oil

1 yellow onion, diced

3 cloves garlic, minced

2 cups vegetable broth

2 tablespoons tomato paste

1 can (15.5 ounces) chickpeas, rinsed and drained

2 cups baby spinach

½ teaspoon red pepper flakes

Salt and freshly ground black pepper

1. Cook pasta according to package directions.

2. Heat olive oil in large skillet over medium-high heat. Add onion and garlic and sauté until onion is soft and translucent, about 5-6 minutes.

3. Add vegetable broth and tomato paste and stir until tomato paste is dissolved. Add chickpeas, spinach, red pepper flakes, salt, and pepper. Cook, stirring occasionally, for 3-4 minutes, until spinach is wilted.

4. Add pasta bows to pan and stir to coat pasta with sauce. Serve hot in bowls.

Rigatoni with Artichokes and Olives

Servings: 4

10 ounces rigatoni

2 tablespoons olive oil

2 cloves garlic, minced

½ onion, chopped

1 jar artichoke hearts, quartered

½ cup black olives, pitted

1 bay leaf

½ teaspoon red pepper flakes

1 cup vegetable broth or water

1 teaspoon dried basil

1 tomato, diced

Salt and black pepper, to taste

1. Cook rigatoni according to package directions.

2. Heat olive oil in large skillet over medium heat. Add garlic and onion and sauté for several minutes until onions are translucent. Add remaining ingredients, stir, lower heat, and simmer for 10 minutes.

3. Place rigatoni in bowls and top with sauce. Serve hot.

Pesto Alfredo Fettucine with Peas

Creamy and delicious, pesto adds a rich flavor to this fettucine alfredo.

Servings: 4

10 ounces fettucine

2 tablespoons olive oil

2 garlic cloves minced

2 tablespoons all-purpose flour

1 ½ cups almond milk

3 tablespoons pesto sauce

½ teaspoon salt

½ teaspoon black pepper

4 tablespoons nutritional yeast

¾ cup green peas

1. Cook fettucine according to package directions, rinse, and set aside.

2. Heat olive oil in large skillet over medium heat.

3. Add garlic and sauté for a minute or two. Add flour and almond milk and stir until flour is dissolved. Lower heat and simmer for 2-3 minutes. Stir in pesto sauce, salt, pepper, and nutritional yeast. Continue simmering, stirring frequently (use whisk to help break up any clumps), until sauce has thickened. Add peas and simmer for 2-3 more minutes until peas are heated through. Add a little more almond milk if sauce gets too thick.

4. Run pasta under hot water and then add to sauce. Toss to thoroughly coat fettucine.

5. Serve hot, with additional salt, pepper, and nutritional yeast, as desired.

Eggplant Casserole

This very tasty dish combines eggplant, potatoes, and assorted vegetables in a delicious casserole.

Servings: 4-5

1 eggplant

1 potato, cut into 1-inch chunks

1 green pepper, diced

1 onion, diced

1 zucchini, cut into slices

1 tomato, diced

½ cup mushrooms, sliced

2 cloves garlic, minced

1 teaspoon dried oregano

1 teaspoon dried basil

1 (15 ounce) can tomato sauce

2 tablespoons olive oil

Salt and freshly ground black pepper, to taste

1. Preheat oven to 400 degrees F.

2. Cut eggplant into 2-inch chunks, spread out on paper-towel lined plate, and sprinkle with salt. Let sit for at least 30 minutes. Rinse under cold water and pat dry with paper towel.

3. Place eggplant in large bowl along with potatoes and the rest of the vegetables. Add seasonings, tomato sauce, olive oil, salt, and pepper. Use large spoon to mix everything together, ensuring all vegetables are covered with seasonings and sauce.

4. Place mixture into large baking dish, cover with aluminum foil, and bake in oven for 2 hours or until vegetables are tender.

Lentil Bolognese

This protein-packed sauce can be served over pasta, rice, or any other grain. The longer it simmers, the better it gets. Tastes great the next day, too.

Servings: 4

1 tablespoon olive oil

2 onions, chopped

2 cloves garlic, minced

1 cup dry lentils, rinsed and drained

1 ½ cups water

2 (14.5 ounce) cans chopped tomatoes

2 vegetable bouillon cubes

1 bay leaf

1 teaspoon dried basil

Salt and black pepper, to taste

1. Heat olive oil in sauce pan over medium high heat. Add onions and garlic and sauté for 5 minutes until onions soften and turn translucent.

2. Add water and lentils to pan and bring to a boil. Cover, reduce heat, and simmer for 20 minutes, until lentils soften.

3. Stir in tomatoes, bouillon cubes, bay leaf, dried basil, salt, and pepper. Simmer, stirring frequently for 15 minutes.

4. Serve over pasta or rice.

SIDE DISHES

The perfect side dish can make the meal.

Here we've collected some of the best.

Broccoli with Ginger

Servings: 2-3

1 bunch broccoli, cut in florets

½ tablespoon fresh ginger, peeled, minced

1 ½ tablespoons olive oil

¼ teaspoon salt

1. In a large saucepan, boil salted water and cook broccoli, uncovered, for about 4 minutes or until tender and crisp. Drain in a colander. Rinse with running water and then transfer in a bowl.

2. In the same pan, heat oil over medium-high heat for about 30 seconds. Stir-fry ginger for about 15 seconds. Mix in broccoli, and cook for another 3 minutes.

Roasted Sweet Potato with Rosemary

2 sweet potatoes, scrubbed, and cubed

½ teaspoon olive oil

1 dash fresh rosemary, finely chopped

1 dash lemon juice

1. Preheat oven to 375 degrees sweFahrenheit.

2. In a bowl, toss sweet potatoes with oil. Evenly spread on a baking sheet, sprinkle with rosemary and roast for about 30 minutes, turning once.

3. Drizzle with lemon juice and serve.

Fried Brussels Sprouts

Servings: 2

½ pound Brussels sprouts, whole

2.5 tablespoon coconut oil

2 garlic cloves, minced

Sea salt to taste

Black pepper to taste

Dash of lemon juice

1. In a pan, heat oil over medium heat. Add whole Brussels sprouts, stir and cook for about 5 minutes or until browned but not charred.

2. Mix in garlic and cook for another minute or until garlic turns light brown. Season with salt and pepper to taste. Drizzle lemon juice. Serve warm.

Garlicky Roasted Cauliflower

Servings: 3

1/8 cup olive oil

1 tablespoon fresh rosemary, minced

½ teaspoon sea salt

¼ teaspoon black pepper

½ large cauliflower, trimmed and cut into bite size pieces

8 cloves garlic, peeled, lightly crushed

Dash of lemon juice

1. Preheat oven to &450 degrees F.

2. In a bowl, combine oil with rosemary, salt, and pepper. Whisk to blend. Add cauliflower, toss to coat. Evenly spread on a baking sheet along with garlic and roast for about 20 minutes. Mix to flip sides, lower temperature to 350 degrees F and cook for another 20 minutes.

3. Served sprinkled with a dash of lemon juice.

Zoodles

Healthy vegetable alternative to noodles that you can use in all your favorite recipes!

Servings: 2

2 medium zucchini

Salt and pepper to taste

1. Using a julienne peeler, cut zucchini into long skinny noodles.

2. These can be cooked by frying in either olive oil or coconut oil for about 2-3 minutes until tender or can be microwaved in a covered, microwavable dish for about 1-2 minutes.

Roasted Carrots with Garlic and Onion

Servings: 2

½ pound baby carrots

1-2 tablespoons olive oil

1-2 green onions, sliced thin

1 garlic clove, minced

Sea salt, to taste

1. Preheat oven to 400 degrees Fahrenheit.

2. In a bowl, toss carrots with olive oil, onions, garlic, and sea salt. Spread carrots in a single layer on parchment or foil-lined baking sheet.

3. Bake for 15-20 minutes or until carrots are tender.

4. Serve.

Roasted Beets and Fennel with Balsamic Glaze

Servings: 2

2 large beets, peeled and cut into chunks

1 stalk fennel, tops cut off and cut into chunks

1/2 medium onion, diced

1/4 cup extra virgin olive oil

1/4 cup balsamic vinegar

Sea salt, to taste

1. Spread beets, fennel, and onion in single layer on a baking sheet.

2. Drizzle olive oil and then vinegar over vegetables. Season with salt. Mix with spoon until vegetables are thoroughly coated.

3. Place in preheated 400 degree F oven for 40-50 minutes or until beets are tender. Turn vegetables every 15 minutes or so while cooking.

4. Serve hot or chilled.

Roasted Balsamic Vegetables

1 tablespoon olive oil

1 garlic clove, minced

1 tablespoon balsamic vinegar

¾ teaspoon fresh rosemary

¼ teaspoon sea salt ½ cup butternut squash, cubed

½ cup broccoli florets, chopped

¼ red onion, chopped

½ zucchini, chopped

1. Preheat oven to 425 degrees F.

2. In a bowl, combine oil, rosemary, vinegar, salt, and pepper; mix to blend. Mix in vegetables, mix to coat evenly. Evenly spread on parchment-lined baking sheet and roast for about 40 minutes or until squash is just softened.

Baby Onions with Balsamic Vinegar

Servings: 3

1 pound baby or pearl onions

2 tablespoons extra-virgin olive oil

½ cup orange juice

¼ cup balsamic vinegar

1. Blanch onions in pot of boiling water for 20 seconds. Remove from water and place in bowl of ice water to cool. When cool, trim ends and peel.

2. In a large skillet, heat olive oil over high heat. Add onions and sauté for 8-10 minutes, until onions begin to brown. Add orange juice and vinegar to pan and bring to boil. Reduce heat to medium-low, cover, and simmer until onions are tender. About 6-7 minutes.

3. Remove onions from pan and place in serving bowl. Continue cooking liquid until it is reduced and has a syrupy consistency. Pour over onions and serve.

Tangy Roasted Broccoli with Garlic

Servings: 2

½ head broccoli, cut into florets

2 cloves garlic, minced

1 teaspoon olive oil

¼ teaspoon sea salt

¼ teaspoon ground black pepper

¼ teaspoon lemon juice

1. In a bowl, combine oil, garlic, salt, and black pepper. Add broccoli. Toss to coat. Evenly scatter broccoli on baking sheet.

2. Place in oven and roast at 350 degrees F for about 10 minutes. Turn florets over and cook for an additional 5-7 minutes or until fork tender.

3. Plate and drizzle with lemon juice. Serve immediately.

Fruit and Vegetable Skewers

Servings: 4

¼ cup olive oil

3 tablespoons lemon juice

1 clove garlic, minced

2 tablespoons parsley, chopped

½ teaspoon salt

½ teaspoon ground black pepper

1 zucchini, cut into slices

1 yellow squash, cut into slices

½ red bell pepper, cut into ½-inch pieces

½ cup cherry tomatoes

½ cup fresh pineapple chunks

4 wooden skewers, soaked for 20-30 minutes in water

1. Mix olive oil, lemon juice, garlic, parsley, salt, and pepper in a bowl. Pour into large sealable plastic bag. Add zucchini, squash, bell pepper, and tomatoes. Seal bag, shake to coat vegetables, and place in refrigerator for a minimum of 1 hour.

2. Remove vegetables from marinade and thread onto skewers, along with pineapple, alternating among each item.

3. Place skewers baking sheet. Cook at 350 degrees F for 8 minutes. Turn skewers over and cook for an additional 6-8 minutes until veggies are desired level of doneness.

4. Remove from oven, transfer to plate, and serve.

Greek-Style Potatoes

Servings: 2

2 large white potatoes

Juice of ½ a lemon

1 tablespoon olive oil

Sea salt and ground black pepper, to taste

½ teaspoon oregano

2 cloves garlic, minced

¼ teaspoon paprika

½ cup vegetable broth

Fresh parsley, chopped, for garnish

1. Cut potatoes in half, then each half into quarters (if potatoes are very large, cut each piece in half again, each slice should be about an inch wide). Place potatoes in large bowl.

2. Add lemon juice, olive oil, salt, pepper, oregano, garlic, and paprika to bowl. Mix well to coat potatoes.

3. Place potatoes into baking dish. Pour vegetable broth over potatoes. Cover with foil.

4. Place pan on 1-inch rack and bake at 350 degrees F for 20-25 minutes until potatoes are tender.

5. Sprinkle with fresh parsley and serve.

Refried Beans

This recipe used canned beans and comes together very quickly,

but tastes like it took all day.

Servings: 4

2 tablespoons olive oil

½ onion, chopped

2 cloves garlic, minced

1 (15 ounce) can pinto beans, undrained

½ teaspoon cumin

Salt and pepper, to taste

1. Heat olive oil in skillet over medium heat. Add onion and garlic and cook, stirring frequently, until onions are softened, about 5 minutes.

2. Add pinto beans and cumin and mash pinto beans using potato masher or back of spoon until beans reach desired consistency.

3. Cook, stirring frequently, for another 4-5 minutes, until beans are heated through. Add salt and pepper to taste.

Garlic Mashed Potatoes

Light and flavorful, these are classic comfort food.

Servings: 4

4 large russet potatoes (about 2 pounds), peeled or unpeeled

6 cloves garlic, minced

3 tablespoons olive oil

3 tablespoons almond milk

Salt and black pepper, to taste

1. Place potatoes and garlic in large pot and cover with water. Add a pinch of salt. Bring to boil and cook, covered, for about 30 minutes, until potatoes are soft. Drain, reserving 1 cup of liquid.

2. Transfer potatoes and garlic to large bowl. Add olive oil, almond milk, salt, and pepper. Mash with potato masher, adding reserved liquid as needed to reach desired consistency.

Fragrant Basmati Rice

1 cup basmati rice

2 cups water

1 tablespoon olive oil

1 onion, sliced

1 teaspoon fresh ginger root, minced (or ¾ teaspoon ground ginger)

¾ cup grated carrots

¼ teaspoon cayenne pepper

½ teaspoon salt

1/3 cup slivered almonds

Chopped fresh cilantro

1. Combine rice and water in sauce. Bring to boil, reduce heat, and simmer, covered, for 20 minutes.

2. While rice is cooking, heat olive oil in skillet over medium heat. Add onion and sauté for 5 minutes until soft. Add in ginger, carrots, cayenne pepper, and salt. Reduce heat to low and cook for another 5 minutes, stirring often.

3. When rice is finished cooking, add to skillet along with slivered almonds and stir to combine all ingredients.

4. Serve garnished with chopped cilantro.

Quinoa and Black Beans

An alternative to the classic black beans and rice.

Servings: 4-6

2 teaspoons olive oil

½ onion, chopped

2 cloves garlic, minced

½ cup quinoa

1 cup vegetable broth

¼ teaspoon cayenne pepper

½ teaspoon salt

½ teaspoon black pepper

½ cup frozen corn kernels

1 can (15 ounce) black beans, rinsed and drained

¼ cup fresh cilantro, chopped

1. Heat oil in saucepan over medium heat. Add onion and garlic, and cook, stirring often, until lightly browned, about 10 minutes.

2. Stir in quinoa, vegetable broth, cayenne pepper, salt, pepper, and corn kernels. Bring to boil, then reduce heat, cover, and simmer until most liquid is absorbed, about 20 minutes.

3. Mix in the black beans and cilantro, and simmer for another 5 minutes.

4. Serve hot.

Moroccan-Style Couscous

Super simple and delicious!

Servings: 3-4

1 cup vegetable broth

1 tablespoon olive oil

½ cup any combination of chopped dates, apricots, raisins

1 cup couscous

1 teaspoon cinnamon

½ cup slivered almonds

1. Add vegetable broth to saucepan and bring to boil. Add olive oil and dried fruit and boil for 2 minutes.

2. Remove from heat, add couscous and cinnamon, stir. Cover and let stand for 4 minutes.

3. Stir in slivered almonds and serve.

Sautéed Mushrooms

Use as a topping for baked potatoes for a simple yet tasty meal.

Servings: 4

3 tablespoons olive oil

2 tablespoons vegan butter

1 pound button mushrooms, washed and sliced

1 clove garlic, minced

1 tablespoon red cooking wine

2 tablespoons teriyaki sauce

Black pepper, to taste

1. Heat olive oil and vegan butter in large skillet over medium heat. When butter is melted add mushroom, garlic, wine, teriyaki sauce, and pepper. Cook, stirring, until mushrooms are browned, about 5 minutes.

2. Reduce heat to low and simmer until mushrooms are tender, about 5 more minutes.

Fried Plantains

A favorite Puerto Rican dish, these can be served with rice and beans.

Servings: 4

Vegetable oil for frying

2 ripe plantains

Salt, to taste

1. Heat oil in large deep skillet over medium-high heat.

2. Peel plantains and slice into thin rounds.

3. Fry plantains in single layer in oil until golden brown. Remove using slotted spoon and dry on paper towels.

4. Season with salt while still warm.

SWEETS

Sometimes you just need a treat. Here you'll find

mouthwatering sweets that are good for you too!

Coconut Date Bites

Simple, sweet, and healthy snack or dessert!

Servings: 4

20 dates, pitted

1 tablespoon coconut butter

1/3 cup coconut flakes

1. In a blender, combine dates with coconut butter; blend until smooth. Form batter into small balls.

2. Roll the balls in the coconut flakes and freeze for 20 minutes.

3. Store in airtight container in refrigerator.

Chocolate Mug Cake

This vegan take on the classic chocolate cake is sure to please.

Servings: 1

¼ cup of sugar

2 teaspoon of unsweetened cocoa powder

¼ cup of flour

¼ teaspoon of baking powder

Pinch of salt

¾ teaspoon of white vinegar

¼ cup of water

½ tablespoon of vegetable oil

¼ teaspoon of vanilla

1. In a large microwave-safe mug, add all dry ingredients.

2. Next add all wet ingredients and stir together.

3. Microwave for 3 minutes on medium power. Voila!

Chia Seed Pudding

Servings: 2

½ cup vanilla almond milk

½ cup vegan yogurt

2 tablespoons maple syrup, divided

½ teaspoon vanilla extract

Pinch of salt

1/8 cup chia seeds

½ pint of strawberries

1/8 cup of almonds (optional)

1. In a bowl add almond milk, yogurt, 1 tablespoon maple syrup, salt, chia seeds, and vanilla.

2. Whisk together until all ingredients are fully distributed.

3. Cover and refrigerate overnight.

4. The next day, in a separate bowl, toss strawberries with 1 tablespoon of maple syrup and add almonds.

5. Spoon pudding into a separate dish, add berry mixture on top and serve.

Peanut Butter Chocolate Nice Cream

Tasty and vegan alternative to traditional ice cream

Servings: 1

1 frozen banana

½ tablespoon cocoa powder

½ tablespoon peanut butter

¼ cup almond milk

1. Add all ingredients into a blender, blend on high until you see a thick creamy consistency and serve.

Baked Stuffed Apples

Great dessert that everyone will love.

Servings: 4

4 large apples

¼ cup coconut flakes

¼ cup dried cranberries or apricots

2 teaspoons orange zest, grated

½ cup orange juice

2 tablespoons brown sugar

1. Cut top off apple and hollow out center with knife or apple corer. Arrange in non-stick baking pan.

2. In a bowl, combine coconut, cranberries, and orange zest. Divide evenly and fill centers of apples.

3. In a bowl, mix orange juice and brown sugar. Pour over apples.

4. Place pan in oven at 350 degrees F and cook 5-6 minutes until apples are tender.

5. Serve warm.

Broiled Peaches

Servings: 2

1 peach

½ tablespoon extra-virgin olive oil

½ tablespoon maple syrup

1. Cut peach in half and remove pit. Brush cut side of peaches with olive oil.

2. Place on parchment-lined pan and place in oven. Cook at 350 degrees F for 5-6 minutes or until peaches are golden brown and caramelized.

3. Drizzle with maple syrup and serve.

Chocolate Zucchini Bread

This moist zucchini bread is a great way to sneak a few extra vegetables in at dessert!

Servings: 1 loaf

2 tablespoons flax meal (to make flegg)

1 cup white sugar

1/6 cup cocoa powder

½ cup vegetable oil

1 cup zucchini, grated

½ teaspoon vanilla extract

1 cup all-purpose flour

½ teaspoon baking soda

½ teaspoon salt

½ teaspoon cinnamon

¼ cup semisweet vegan chocolate chips

1. Spray a 9 x 5 inch loaf pan with cooking spray.

2. Combine flaxseed with 6 tablespoons of hot water in small bowl. This is an egg substitute known as "flegg."

3. In a large mixing bowl, sugar, cocoa powder, oil, grated zucchini, vanilla, and flegg. Beat well. Stir in flour, baking soda, salt, and cinnamon. Stir in chocolate chips.

4. Pour batter into prepared pans. Bake at 350 degrees F for 40-45 minutes until knife inserted in center comes out clean. Let bread rest inside dome for 1-2 minutes before removing from oven. Allow to cool before slicing.

Apple and Strawberry Crumble

Servings: 4

2 apples, peeled, small pieces

2 cups strawberries, halved

½ cup sugar

1 cup oats

1 cup coconut milk

½ cup pistachios

½ cup coconut powder

1. Preheat oven at 350 degrees.

2. In a blender add oats, sugar, coconut milk, pistachios and blend for 1-2 minutes.

3. Take a large bowl add strawberries, apples, oats mixture and toss to combine.

4. Transfer into serving dish and sprinkle coconut powder on top and bake for 25 minutes.

5. Serve and enjoy.

Non-Dairy Chocolate Pudding

Creamy and chocolatey good!

Servings: 4

1 banana, sliced

1 package (12 ounces) soft silken tofu

¼ cup confectioners' sugar

5 tablespoons cocoa powder, unsweetened

3 tablespoons coconut milk (or soy)

½ teaspoon ground cinnamon

1. Place all ingredients in blender and blend until smooth. Pour into individual dishes, chill in refrigerator for at least 1 hour.

Oatmeal Cookies with Cranberries and Chia Seeds

Healthy and easy to make, these are good for a sweet treat or even breakfast on the go.

Servings: 12 cookies

2 cups rolled oats

2/3 cup all-purpose or whole-wheat flour

1 cup brown sugar, lightly packed

1 teaspoon ground cinnamon

1 teaspoon baking soda

½ teaspoon baking powder

½ teaspoon salt

2 tablespoons chia seeds

½ cup applesauce

3 tablespoons coconut oil

¾ cup dried cranberries

1. Preheat oven to 350 degrees F.

2. In mixing bowl, combine oats, flour, brown sugar, cinnamon, baking soda, baking powder, salt, and chia seeds. Mix in applesauce and coconut oil. Fold in cranberries.

3. Spoon dough onto parchment lined baking sheet.

4. Bake for 12-14 minutes, until cookies are golden brown. Cool on wire rack.

Popcorn Drizzled with Chocolate and Pistachios

This is an easy treat to make up for a party.

Servings: 6-8

7 cups popped popcorn

½ cup vegan semi-sweet chocolate chips

½ cup pistachios, shelled and chopped

1. Spread popcorn in single layer on baking sheet

2. Place chocolate chips in microwave safe bowl. Heat in microwave in 30-second intervals, stirring each time, until melted.

3. Drizzle chocolate over popcorn using spoon. Sprinkle with pistachio nuts. Let sit until chocolate hardens.

4. Serve at once or store in airtight container.

Chocolate Peanut Butter Fudge

An easy and decadent treat.

Servings: 12

1 cup vegan semi-sweet chocolate chips

1 cup peanut butter

¾ cup maple syrup

1. Place chocolate chips in microwave safe bowl. Microwave in 30 second intervals until chips are melted. Stir in peanut butter and maple syrup, and stir until smooth.

2. Pour into parchment-lined baking dish. Chill in refrigerator for 5 hours or overnight. Cut into 12 pieces.

Cherry Crisp

So yummy! Serve with whipped coconut cream or vegan ice cream.

Servings: 6

1 can (21 ounce) cherry pie filling

½ cups rolled oats

½ cup all-purpose flour

1 teaspoon cinnamon

½ teaspoon nutmeg

1/3 cup vegan butter, melted

½ cup walnuts, chopped

1. Preheat oven to 375 degrees F. Spray 2-quart baking dish with nonstick cooking spray. Spread cherry pie filling evenly in pan.

2. Mix together oats, flour, cinnamon, nutmeg, and melted butter. Spread over pie filling and top with chopped walnuts.

3. Bake for 25-30 minutes until golden brown.

Snickerdoodles

Easy and delicious!

Servings: 12 cookies

1 ½ cups whole wheat flour

½ cup sugar + ¼ cup sugar

½ teaspoon salt

½ teaspoon baking soda

½ cup vegetable oil

½ cup applesauce

1 tablespoon vanilla extract

2 tablespoons almond milk

1 teaspoon cinnamon

1. Preheat oven to 375 degrees F.

2. In mixing bowl, combine flour, ½ cup sugar, salt, and baking soda. Beat in oil, applesauce, vanilla extract, and almond milk.

3. Roll dough in 12 equal size balls.

4. In shallow bowl, mix together remaining ¼ cup sugar and cinnamon. Roll dough balls in sugar mixture and arrange on parchment lined cookie sheet.

5. Bake for 10-11 minutes until golden brown. Cook on wire rack.

From the Author

Thank you for reading *The Vegan College Cookbook.* I sincerely hope that you found this book informative and helpful and that it helps you to create delicious foods for yourself, friends, and family.

Happy cooking!

INDEX

More Bestselling Titles from Dylanna Press

***Mason Jar Meals* by Dylanna Press**

Mason jar meals are a fun and practical way to take your meals on the go. Mason jars are an easy way to prepare individual servings, so whether you're cooking for one, two, or a whole crowd, these fun, make-ahead meals will work.

Includes More than 50 Recipes and Full-Color Photos

In this book, you'll find a wide variety of recipes including all kinds of salads, as well as hot meal ideas such as mini chicken pot pies and lasagna in a jar. Also included are mouth-watering desserts such as strawberry shortcake, apple pie, and s'mores.

The recipes are easy to prepare and don't require any special cooking skills. So what are you waiting for? Grab your Mason jars and start preparing these gorgeous and tasty dishes!

The Inflammation Diet by Dylanna Press

Beat Pain, Slow Aging, and Reduce Risk of Heart Disease with the Inflammation Diet

Inflammation has been called the "silent killer" and it has been linked to a wide variety of illnesses including heart disease, arthritis, diabetes, chronic pain, autoimmune disorders, and cancer.

Often, the root of chronic inflammation is in the foods we eat.

The Inflammation Diet: Complete Guide to Beating Pain and Inflammation will show you how, by making simple changes to your diet, you can greatly reduce inflammation in your body and reduce your symptoms and lower your risk of chronic disease.

The book includes a complete plan for eliminating inflammation and implementing an anti-inflammatory diet:

• Overview of inflammation and the body's immune response – what can trigger it and why chronic inflammation is harmful
• The link between diet and inflammation
• Inflammatory foods to avoid
• Anti-inflammatory foods to add to your diet to beat pain and inflammation
• Over 50 delicious inflammation diet recipes
• A 14-day meal plan

Take charge of your health and implement the inflammation diet to lose weight, slow the aging process, eliminate chronic pain, and reduce the likelihood and symptoms of chronic disease.

Learn how to heal your body from within through diet.

DASH Diet Slow Cooker Recipes by Dylanna Press

Delicious and Healthy DASH Diet Recipes for Your Slow Cooker

The DASH diet has once again been named the healthiest diet by top nutrition experts and there's no better time to start reaping the rewards of this smart, sensible eating plan. Eating the DASH diet way does not have to be boring, in fact, it contains the most delicious foods around – lean meats, whole grains, lots of fresh fruits and vegetables, and flavorful herbs and spices. So whether you are just starting out on the DASH diet or have been eating low-sodium for years, the *DASH Diet Slow Cooker Recipes: Easy, Delicious, and Healthy Recipes* is going to help you make delicious, healthy meals without spending a lot of time in the kitchen.

For this book, we've collected the best slow cooker recipes and adapted them to the DASH diet to create mouthwatering, family-pleasing dishes that can all be prepared easily and then cooked in your slow cooker while you're off doing other things. There's really nothing better than coming home at the end of a hectic day to the smell of tonight's dinner already prepared and waiting to be eaten.

These recipes feature fresh, whole foods and include a wide variety of recipes to appeal to every taste from classic dishes to new twists that just may become your new favorites. In addition, each recipe has less than 500 mg of sodium per serving, many a lot less than that.

In addition to recipes, the book includes a brief overview of the DASH diet as well as tips on how to get the most out of your slow cooker.

Dump Dinners: Amazingly Easy and Delicious Dump Recipes by Julia Grady

With the hectic pace of today's lifestyles getting dinner on the table every night is no easy task. When pressed for time, dump dinners make the perfect solution to the question, What's for dinner?

Dump dinners are so popular because they are so easy to make.

These recipes feature simple ingredients that you probably already have on hand in your freezer, refrigerator, and pantry. They do not require complicated cooking techniques or that you stand over the stove, stirring and sautéing. The majority of the recipes are mixed right in the pan they are cooked in, with the added bonus of saving cleanup time.

Delicious, Quick Recipes Your Family Will Love

This book contains the best dump dinner recipes around. None of these recipes take more than 15 minutes of hands-on time to prepare, and most a lot less. When you're short on time, you can turn to any one of these delicious recipes and have a home-cooked meal on the table with little effort and big rewards.

The recipes in this book can be cooked in several ways:
- Baked in the oven
- Cooked in a slow cooker
- Cooked on the stovetop
- Microwaved
- Frozen and cooked later

So whether you'd like to throw something in the slow cooker and come home hours later to an aromatic meal or pop a quickly prepared casserole into the oven, you are sure to find a recipe you and your family will love.

18320374R00108

Printed in Poland
by Amazon Fulfillment
Poland Sp. z o.o., Wrocław